EASY PC

EASY PC

HOW TO USE YOUR FIRST COMPUTER

Dr Kenneth Mole
with Mike Hobbs

RIGHT WAY

Constable & Robinson Ltd
3 The Lanchesters
162 Fulham Palace Road
London W6 9ER

www.constablerobinson.com

First published in the UK 2000

This completely revised and updated edition published by
Right Way, an imprint of Constable & Robinson, 2008

2

A copy of the British Library Cataloguing in Publication Data is
available from the British Library

ISBN: 978-0-7160-2193-3

Printed and bound in the EU

Thanks to Claire Welch for her contribution.

FSC
Mixed Sources
Product group from well-managed
forests and other controlled sources

Cert no. SGS - COC - 2061
www.fsc.org
© 1996 Forest Stewardship Council

CONTENTS

ACKNOWLEDGEMENTS

Acknowledgement is made to the following companies and products mentioned in this book, many of which are registered as trademarks:

Microsoft Corporation

Microsoft ® Windows XP

Microsoft ® Windows Vista

Microsoft ® WordPad

Microsoft ® Paint

Microsoft ® Outlook Express

INTRODUCTION

'Easy' manuals for beginners, written by experts, are baffling because experts have forgotten what it was like to be beginners. It is true that computing is easy, but only when explained to a beginner by a beginner.

So I began writing this guide from the moment I first sat down to my first computer. In no time at all, you too will be word-processing, managing documents, drawing pictures, e-mailing and web surfing with ease. There's a wonderful world out there!

The basic machinery you need is a PC (Personal Computer) equipped with Windows XP or Windows Vista, a printer, some **floppy disks** and loudspeakers. There is a screen (the **monitor**) and a keyboard for typing. There is a slot or drawer, also known as a drive window, where a **compact disc** (a CD or CD-ROM) fits when you press the button underneath it, and a smaller slot into which a floppy disk fits. Try them out for size. Your PC may also take DVDs (Digital Versatile Discs – super CD-ROMs which can produce games, movies and surround sound) in the same slot as CDs. On some PCs you can put 'blank' discs into the slot and store information on them.

Many people with a 14 inch monitor wish they'd spent a little more on a larger one. A 17 inch one gives almost a 50 per cent bigger screen area. I'm glad I splashed out and changed my 14 inch one for a 17 inch. A flat-panel monitor will save you a great deal of desk space.

When your new PC arrives, someone knowledgeable must do the installation for you and give a basic demonstration of how it all works. However, one and a half seconds after they've left the room, your mind will revert to a blind blank. At least ask your installer how to switch on and how to switch off. (If you forget how to switch off, read page 31.) Dealers busy installing their wares can't be expected to spare time teaching in detail: that's why you need this book.

Have a printer installed for you from the beginning, as fitting one can be daunting. For using the internet or e-mail you need to have a telephone socket within easy reach.

Words like *compact disc, monitor or scanner*, which may need further explanation, are found in the index at the end of this book. They are printed in **bold** type (unless they are sub-headings) and you can expect further explanation if you look them up in the index, and they stand out clearly when you turn from the index to the page to which the index refers. MAKE A HABIT OF USING THE INDEX: IT'S YOUR BEST FRIEND!

Because one PC differs from another, what appears on your screen may differ slightly from what's described in this book – different colours for instance, or minor variations in procedure. Do not worry about minor differences.

This book was first published in 2000. Since then, of

course, new operating systems have been introduced. This new edition has been thoroughly updated to cover both Windows XP and Windows Vista. However, as I do not use Windows Vista, Mike Hobbs has kindly written the new section on that.

Dr Kenneth Mole

PART ONE

WINDOWS XP

EXERCISE 1

SINGLE-CLICKING

Switch on by pressing what is probably the largest button on the front of the PC. (You may need to switch on the monitor as well.) Your floppy disk slot should be empty. If it isn't, a message may appear on the screen saying something like **non-system disk or disk error**, so you're already in trouble, but you can get out of it. Remove the disk (by pressing the button near the floppy disk slot) and then press **any key** on your keyboard as, if you look carefully, your screen will tell you to do.

After various unintelligible messages have come and gone, your screen stops changing. What it now shows is called your **Desktop**. It is what you now see on your monitor: a coloured background on which are scattered little pictures called Icons, each labelled underneath with a name.

Look for the name **My Computer**. We shall now change that name, not because it strikes some people as tacky, but because we shall learn a lot in the process of changing it.

The end of your mouse farthest away from you has two Buttons you can press, a right one and a left one. (Some have three Buttons, or a little wheel as well.) Get your mouse pointer to rest on the name **My Computer** pictured below:

My Computer

Now *press and release* the left mouse Button. That press and release action is called clicking. **My Computer** will become highlighted, changing colour:

My Computer

Your colours may vary, but highlighting will be obvious. Left-click again. The name box now incorporates a **cursor**, a vertical bar that blinks:

My Computer

Alternatively, a single right-click produces a Menu with **Rename** on it:

Open
Explore
Search...
Manage
Map Network Drive...
Disconnect Network Drive...
Create Shortcut
Delete
Rename
Properties

Left-click **Rename** and the cursor will start blinking. When something blinks at you, it is an invitation for you to start typing. In fact, you can't type anything anywhere unless you are invited to do so by having something **blink** at you.

Now type on your keyboard a new name, say **the whole shebang**. (You may need the backspace key ◄——— on your keyboard to delete a mistyped letter.) This changes the name to:

the whole
shebang|

As confirmation, left-click your ⬚ in an empty space on the icon-littered screen – your Desktop. **The whole shebang** will become highlighted.

the whole shebang

Left-clicks are much more often used than right-clicks, so from now on, if I say 'click', I mean *left*-click unless otherwise stated.

Click again on a blank bit of Desktop and it will become inactive, unhighlighted. To change the name back to what it was in the first place, click on it to highlight it, and then click again to make it blink. Type in the letters **My Computer**.

My Computer|

Click on the Desktop twice: once to confirm the name and once to unhighlight it. You're back to where you started:

My Computer

If you've had any difficulty so far, it's probably because the mouse moved when you clicked it. Cultivate a secure touch – don't jiggle as you click. It may stray because your hand is shaking with excitement or from old age. Many beginners' frustrations are due to wobbling. Perhaps children are computer naturals because they have small fingers.

A Summary of Exercise 1

Switch on. Put your mouse arrow on the name **My Computer**. Click to highlight it. Click again to make it blink. Type **the whole shebang**. Click on the Desktop to confirm. Click again on the Desktop to get it off duty, unhighlighted.

To reverse the process, you clicked **the whole shebang** to highlight it, making it ready for action, and clicked it again to make it blink. You typed **My Computer**, then clicked on the Desktop as confirmation and finished by clicking again on the Desktop to get **My Computer** unhighlighted, off duty. The Desktop is now back to where it started and you now know how to click.

If, at this point, you want to take a break for a cup of tea, have a quick look at page 31 for details of how to shut down the computer safely.

EXERCISE 2

DOUBLE-CLICKING

My Computer

With the Desktop showing on your screen, point your mouse arrow onto the **My Computer** icon – the little image of a monitor and computer – and click. The icon and its name become highlighted meaning, "We have been chosen for action". Click again and nothing happens. That's because in order to see what's represented by an icon you have to double-click, i.e. click it twice in very quick succession. This opens it up to show what it's the symbol for. Double-clicking takes practice. If you get it right, a window appears, called in its top left-hand corner by the same name as the icon you double-clicked – in this case **My Computer**. (To get rid of a window, to **close** it, click the ☒ in the top right-hand corner.) If you've got the **My Computer** window in front of you click its ☒. Then practise opening the **My Computer** window again by double-clicking the **My Computer** icon or its name on the Desktop. You can double-click the icon or its name; it makes no difference. The name is tied to its icon like a luggage label. The difference is only important when you want to single-click on the label in order to change its name. Practise shutting the window by clicking the ☒ and opening it again.

If you find double-clicking difficult, there are two solutions. The first is to click just once and then press **Enter** ◂——┘ on the keyboard. That works in the same way as a double-click and is easier for beginners. The second solution is to alter the timing of the double-click. You may not need to do this, but the process of doing so is instructive. For this, click the **Start Button** 🏁 start , seen on the left-hand bottom corner of your screen.

When you put your mouse arrow on 🏁 start the words "Click here to begin" may appear, but you can ignore that. It's just your machine trying to be helpful. Click 🏁 start and a **Menu** appears divided into two columns of icons. It may look bewildering at first but we'll return to the **Start** menu so often that you'll soon get used to where things are.

Briefly, the column on the right shows all sorts of useful folders and tools in one place so that you don't have to go searching around for them each time. The column on the left lists programs – and only programs – divided into two sections by a thin line. The programs in the top section remain there, always available for you to click and start using them. Below the thin line are your most frequently used programs, opened and ready to use with just a single click. Clicking **All Programs**, at the very bottom, shows a list of all programs on your computer. (To get rid of a Menu, click anywhere except on the Menu itself or on an icon.)

Now move your mouse arrow, without clicking upwards over the Menu, passing over the icons in the right-hand column until it has arrived over **Control Panel** which will turn darker as you reach it.

That means it is operational, on duty, at your service. Click it and it will open. (On a Menu, a single-click selects an item.)

Among the two dozen or so items shown in that **Control Panel** window – in alphabetical order – is one called **Mouse**. To see what it is, put your ⌖ on it and double-click. If you have clicked correctly, an **egg-timer** ⧖ may momentarily appear – a request that you should wait a moment. (Instead of double-clicking, you can of course click just once and press the **Enter** key on the keyboard.)

This double-click opens the **Mouse** item on the **Control Panel** window to reveal what it stands for, the **Mouse Properties** window.

Put your ▷ over the slider between **Slow** and **Fast**, press the left clicker and, keeping it pressed down, move the mouse sideways. The slider will also move.

```
┌─ Double Click Speed ────────────────────────────────────────────┐
│   Double-click the folder to test your setting.  If the folder does not    ┌─────────┐   │
│   open or close, try using a slower setting.                               │         │   │
│                                                                            │   📁    │   │
│          Slow ─────────┤────── Fast                                        │         │   │
│               ı ı ı ı ı ı ı ı ı ı ı ı                                      └─────────┘   │
└──────────────────────────────────────────────────────────────────┘
```

By doing this you can alter the double-click speed from **Fast** to **Slow**. Moving something in this way, by moving the mouse with a clicker pressed, is called **dragging**.

This fiddling with double-click speeds may seem a triviality, but by playing with the Mouse Properties window we can learn a lot about many other windows we shall come across. Note, for instance, the **question mark** at the top right-hand corner of the Mouse Properties window. This appears on several windows. Click the ? and release the clicker. When you move your mouse the ? will now move as well. Move the ? to the folder icon 📁 to the right of the slider. Now click again. The answer to your question now appears – it should be something like this:

```
┌──────────────────────────────────────────────────────────────┐
│  Double-click here to test the double-click speed of your primary  │
│  button. If the folder opens or closes, the double-click was       │
│  recognized.                                                       │
└──────────────────────────────────────────────────────────────┘
```

(To get rid of a message, click elsewhere on the Mouse Properties window.) Move your mouse arrow into the test area and double-click. If you've got it right, the folder opens up ☞. To close it, double-click again. Try clicking the ? again and moving it to Switch primary and secondary buttons and clicking it there. The answer it gives is:

> Clear the check box if you are right-handed and the left mouse button is the one you use most often. Select the check box if you are left-handed and use the right mouse button most often. The picture at the right indicates the selected primary mouse button.

The next few paragraphs are tricky, the only difficult ones in this whole book, but persevere. If you are left-handed and want to change your mouse so that you can use your left hand to work it, read what follows very carefully. If you don't want to make a change, it's worth reading all the same, because you'll learn something useful.

The dot in a white circle ⊙, which you can see next to **Switch primary and secondary buttons** on the **Mouse Properties** window, marks an option which has been chosen. A circle without a dot in it ◯ marks an **option** which has not been chosen. A window with one black dotted circle and other un-dotted ones is called a **dialogue box**. (You may have a white square with a green tick instead.)

Try changing the **default** or pre-selected option, which is **Right-handed** (pre-selected by your machine because most people are right-handed), by moving your mouse arrow to the Switch primary and secondary buttons white dot and clicking that. Sure enough, the black dot now appears there, and you should now transfer the mouse to your left hand

and use your left forefinger on the right mouse Button for ordinary clicking. If you want to keep things left-handed you must click **Apply** and then **OK.** To revert to the right-handed option, move your mouse arrow to the Switch primary and Secondary buttons white circle and click there. The white circle is no longer marked with a black dot. Often the white circle is referred to as a 'check box'! One with a black dot in it is 'checked'; without a tick it is 'un-checked'. All this is obvious to children and computers, who are more logical than grown-ups whose intuition can get them into terrible Windows frustration.

One moral of that treacherous paragraph is that much beginner's bewilderment is due to the machine being under orders which are not appreciated by its operator. Sometimes this is due to ignorance or forgetfulness, sometimes to a misplaced mouse or mistyped key. Occasionally a **gremlin** is the only possible explanation. For hints on getting out of trouble see STUCK! in the index.

Another moral is that you must be on the look-out for **OK, Apply** and similar suggestions, because you won't be able to progress unless you play your part by responding. You may, for instance, at various times be invited to click **Yes, No, OK, Apply, Cancel, Done, Close, Quit, Display, Exit** or whatever is offered. You're stuck until you respond.

There is another lesson here. The screen may often be full of stuff you can't or don't need to understand, but make a habit of glancing all over it. There may be something there that will save you hours of frustration, something as simple as clicking an **OK** you hadn't noticed.

Before we can get on to anything more serious, there is another lesson to be learnt from the Mouse Properties window. At the top you will see what are called **tabs**. Many windows have them. This window has four or five of them, **Buttons, Pointers, Pointer Options, Wheel and Hardware**. Click each one in turn and glance at what is offered – mostly unimportant. The lesson here is that you must not try to digest everything that a window offers; you must learn to select only what you need.

Here is a summary of the steps you have taken so far in Exercise 2. Move to **Start**. Click. Move up to **Control Panel** Control Panel and click. Choose **Mouse** and double-click. Drag the slider to **Slow** and confirm by clicking **OK**. The Mouse Properties window may close by itself, but if not click its to close it. Click on the Control Panel window to close that one also.

In short: start – Control Panel – **Mouse – Slow – OK** – to the Desktop.

Icons

With Windows, almost everything has a little **icon** plonked beside it, but you will find that you can safely look at the name of an item, not its icon. There were a good twenty icons on the **Control Panel** window you had open just now, but you chose **Mouse** because it was spelt that way, not because of its icon (a little picture of a computer mouse). Icons come into their own when sitting on little Buttons too small to have their names on. We meet buttons in the next exercise.

EXERCISE 3

MANIPULATING WINDOWS

Whatever occupies your screen – be it your Desktop, a window or several windows – a bar will show, usually on the bottom edge.

start

This, recognizable by the oblong **Start Button** on its left, is the **taskbar**. (If it's not there, follow what is in the Index under taskbar not present.)

If you put your mouse arrow � over the taskbar and press and keep pressed the left clicker, you can drag the taskbar to any edge of the screen. It is usually at the bottom but some people like it at the top. Here are some other tricks:

1. Starting from the Desktop, double-click **My Computer** (or click it once to highlight it and press the **Enter** key). The **My Computer** window then appears:

| ⚡ My Computer | | ⎽ ⧉ ✕ |

At the right-hand end of its title-bar are three little Buttons. If the middle one is ⧉ , as in the picture above, put your ⬚ on it and click. The **My Computer** window will shrink. This can be useful when you want to make room for something else on your screen. (When you shrink a window, the ⧉ Button changes to ◻ .) If the middle one is, ◻ , click it and the window expands to occupy the whole screen. Clicking ◻ is called **maximizing a window**. When it's maximized, the middle of the three Buttons changes back from ◻ to ⧉ , ready for shrinking, in case that's what you want.

Now click the left Button, ⎽ . The window becomes **minimized**, collapsing to the taskbar, where it remains represented by an oblong Button labelled with its icon and its name, **My Computer**.

| 🏁 **start** | ⚡ My Computer |

Minimizing is a way of putting a window temporarily out of the way. You will see that the Buttons go in and out when clicked. By clicking on that **My Computer** Button on the taskbar you can bring the **My Computer** window back to occupy the screen. Then shrink it.

2. Put your mouse arrow ⬚ into the title-bar at the top of the **My Computer** window and, holding down the clicker, move the arrow about with your mouse. This is known as **dragging a window about**. When you release the clicker, the window stays in its new position.

If you're stuck with a window with its title-bar missing, with no ☒ to click, click on any sliver of its title-bar at the top of the screen. You can then drag the window down or to the left for the ☒ to show up again.

3. Point your ⇖ carefully and accurately at any of the four edges of a shrunken window. Don't press the clicker until the ⇖ changes into a **double-headed arrow**↕. You can then drag that edge in any direction, altering the size and shape of the window. You can do the same sort of thing if you land accurately on a corner.

Your next trick shows you how to manage several windows at a time. ☒ away any open windows so as to have a clear Desktop. Click 🏁 start . Move your ⇖ up to Control Panel and click. Make sure that the Control Panel window is shrunk (by pressing the 🗗, if available), then put your ⇖ into the title-bar of the Control Panel window and drag it to a lower part of the screen.

Click 🏁 start again and go up to Settings again. This time go over to Printers and Faxes and click and shrink that. Drag the window's title-bar down to the lower part of the screen, on top of the Control Panel window. Click 🏁 start a third time and go up to Search and click that. Drag the Search Results window down, like the others, to make more room on your screen. You now have three windows open, Control Panel, Printers and Faxes and Search Results.

Each open window is represented by a Button on the taskbar:

🏁 start | 📁 Control Panel | 🖨 Printers and Faxes | 🔍 Search Results

A click on one of those taskbar Buttons jumps its window up to the front of the screen. Click on another and the window which that one represents will also open up, in front of the previous one. Try it. This is a useful manoeuvre for **switching from one window to another** when you're working on more than one window at the same time.

When you close a window by ▣ing it, its Button on the taskbar disappears. You can close a window represented on the taskbar by clicking its Button there and ▣ing it when it opens up. You can also close it by a **right-click on its Button on the taskbar** and choosing Close.

You can make the **taskbar thicken**, to give it more space for the name of the windows, by putting the mouse arrow over its upper edge, waiting for the ↕ to appear, and then dragging upwards, but it's good practice to keep your taskbar uncluttered.

4. You now have three windows open. Click a bit of window lurking behind others and that window will come to the front. Try clicking on each window in turn.

The taskbar, being only as wide as your screen, has to use **abbreviations** when it has to show on it more names of windows than it can spell out in full. It then gives a shortened version of the name followed by full stops... To see the full name of such an abbreviation, rest your ⯭ for a second on the abbreviated version and the full name will appear.

5. If you right-click on a blank bit of taskbar a Menu appears with the command Cascade Windows, among others. Click that and your three messy windows will arrange themselves neatly.

You can bring one of your choice to the front by clicking on a bit of it, or by clicking on its Button on the taskbar, as I have done here with **Search Results**. Cascaded windows have a neat line of 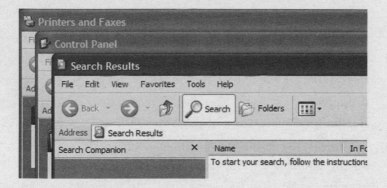s which are easy to click.

6. A right-click on the taskbar will offer **Show the Desktop**. This is useful for revealing your **Desktop**. (Even better is the icon , present on some taskbars, a click on which will reveal your Desktop.) You can restore minimized windows by clicking them one by one on the taskbar or you can right-click on the taskbar again and click **Undo Minimize All**.

If the **taskbar has disappeared** below the bottom of the screen, put your over the bottom of the screen until the double-headed arrow appears. This may take patience. Keeping the clicker pressed, drag upwards. When the taskbar is showing, clicking the start Button can display the **Start Menu** in front of any windows that may be open.

Don't try to learn all of this exercise. Use the index and refer back to items printed in bold. Don't try to remember when to single-click (which is to *single* things out for attention) and when to double-click (which is to *open* things up). You will soon remember what comes in useful to you and forget the rest. You will, however, gradually come automatically to remember a few **right-clicks**. Some are listed in the Index.

EXERCISE 4

SHUTTING DOWN

After a few minutes, whatever is showing on screen may be replaced by an image called a **screen saver**. If your screen saver is in action and you want to restore your screen, jiggle the mouse.

To get rid of your screen saver, go **Start – Control Panel – Display** – click the **Screen Saver** tab. In the **Screen Saver** box click on the ▾ to bring up a list of options, and scroll to find **None**. Select **None** and click **OK**. If you want to have fun with a personalized screen saver, click the **Screen Saver** tab and, instead of **None**, select, say, **Marquee** if available. Click **Settings**. Choose a **Background Color**. Type in, say, **Just don't PANIC, Geraldine**. Click **OK** on that window and **OK** again on the next window. ☒ away the Control Panel window, wait, and you'll see **Just don't PANIC, Geraldine** scrolling up. (Computers vary on the details of this procedure, so don't worry if it doesn't work first time for you.)

When you want to shut down your computer, you must

check that all programs are shut. So empty your taskbar of any Buttons showing program names there by right-clicking and selecting **Close**. Then go to , on the left end of the *taskbar*, click, move up to **Turn off Computer**, the next item above it, and click that. In the **Turn off Computer** window which then appears, click the red button, **Turn off** and that should be it. It's good practice to switch off your monitor too.

When should you switch off your machine? The experts don't agree about that. Some people don't turn their computers off, ever. They say that keeping the temperature constant is a Good Thing, as it is for storing wine, and that constant wear and tear from switching on and off is a Bad Thing. Other people say it is a Bad Thing to leave it on all the time because the monitor wears and the computer's components get overheated. I turn mine off at night, if only to remove that telltale gleam from the curtains. As a further burglar precaution I also switch off when leaving the house.

EXERCISE 5

CHOOSING PROGRAMS

Switch on. Click **start** on the taskbar. Go up to **All Programs**. Wait half a second and the names of programs appear. To get rid of this **Start Menu**, click anywhere else on the screen and you're back to the Desktop.

Begin again with **start**, go up again to **All Programs**. (To choose an item on a Menu, single it out with a single-click.) After waiting that half second, a vast Menu of programs appears on the right, where the arrowhead is pointing. There's an extremely wide choice because many of them have arrowheads themselves, pointing to even more programs. If you move your ⌖ to rest on an item with an arrowhead ▸, the names of the programs to which it is pointing will appear. You can then click on the program of your choice. Many of these you will never use, so don't be dismayed because there are so many of them.

When the programs to which **All Programs** is pointing appear, go up near the top, to **Games**. Sure enough, after half a second, what that arrowhead is pointing to appears.

Go horizontally to the selection of games offered, not because it's playtime but because we'll learn a lot by doing so. Click **Solitaire**, the card game many of us know as Patience.

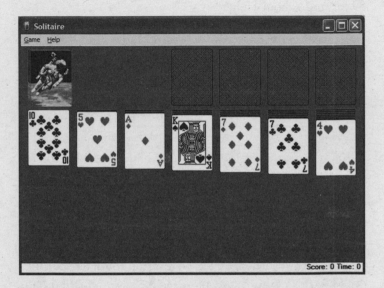

You play Solitaire by **dragging and dropping** the cards about. To drag and drop something, point on it with your mouse arrow, press down the left clicker and, keeping it pressed, move the mouse about. The object that you pointed at will move also. That's the *dragging* action. When it is where you want it, release the clicker. That's the *dropping* action. To practise dragging and dropping, try moving a few cards about in this way. If they don't want to stay where you put them, that's only because the rules of the game say they can't.

To read those rules, point to the word **Help**, which shows just beneath the window's title, **Solitaire**, and click. Go down to **Contents,** click that and a Help window opens where you can find out all about the game. Many windows have a Help window or 'Viewer', the topics dealt with being relevant to the subject of that particular window (see page 89 for more about Help).

You can now choose to play Solitaire, to ⊠ the window away, to shrink it, to minimize it down to the taskbar, or to forget about it until the time comes to switch off, when you must make sure the window is closed.

This time, forget about it and profit from the way you can leave stuff on your screen and press on regardless. This is thanks to the constant availability of the **Start** Button on the taskbar for starting something else and from the fact that the most recently opened window always shows up in front of earlier ones. The limitation is that an overburdened computer slows down.

So press 🏁 start and go again to **All Programs – Games.** This time click **Hearts.** A window called **The Microsoft Hearts Network** shows. I see on my version of this window that my nephew has been there before me and typed in his name, so I just click **OK** so as to press on, but you can type in your own name if none appears. This opens a window full of playing cards. Click **Help – Help Topics** and then click on the little symbol of a book labelled Hearts under the Contents tab. From the list that appears click on Play Hearts. Ignore the details of **Play Hearts** in the right-hand pane of the window, but just notice that there is more in this window than can be contained in one screen's worth. The problem is overcome by a **scroll bar**. The Hearts Help window has a vertical scroll bar on its right edge. At its bottom is an arrowhead 🔽 pointing downwards and at its top is one pointing upwards 🔼. Between the two is a **slider** which you can click and drag up or down like a lift in a lift-shaft. When a window contains a document even 100 or more pages long, by dragging the slider you can move over all of it with fantastic speed. One click on an arrowhead moves you up or down a line. A click just above or below the slider scrolls a whole screen's length.

Some windows provide a horizontal scroll bar at the bottom, with ◀ and ▶ for clicking and a slider for dragging, so as to reveal what's on either side of the screen to right or left.

When a window has two panes, you can enlarge one pane at the expense of the other by resting your ⌖ on the interface between the two and waiting for it to change to a double arrow ◀▶ and then dragging sideways.

Now clear your screen of windows by clicking any ❎ so as to get back to the Desktop ready for the next exercise. Or, you can get the same result by clearing your taskbar with a right-click on any Button there and clicking **Close**.

EXERCISE 6

WORD-PROCESSING

6.i WordPad

```
Document - WordPad
File  Edit  View  Insert  Format  Help

Arial            10    Western           B  /  U  ☺  ▣ ☰ ☰  ☷

X··1··2··3··4··5··6··7··8··9··10··11··12··13··14··



                    Blank page for typing|




For Help, press F1
```

On a typewriter, what you type is often called a 'document'.
In a word-processing program on your computer you can also
type a **document,** but, in computer-speak, it is usually called
a File.

The word **'File'** is computer jargon, often inter-
changeable with the word 'document'. In ordinary speech,
a File is a box or folder for holding a number of individual

items stored under the same name. In computer-speak, however, a File may be not a *collection* of items stored under one name, but just one *single* item. And, furthermore, a File may be words on a page, a blank page, a chapter of a book, a whole book, a photograph, a set of instructions, a recording of music or a mixture of any such items.

The computer-speak name for a *collection* of Files is a **Folder**. Another name for a Folder is a **Directory**. You'll soon get used to this jargon and find yourself speaking it like a native.

We shall now type a document or, in other words, create a File. To do this we first have to find somewhere in which to type it. Your computer provides this, a program designed for this purpose, a blank page called WordPad.

This is the name of the most basic word-processing program offered by Windows. It has its weaknesses – it can type only in **single-spacing** and it can't count words or check spelling – so you may want to add to your PC a better system by buying some extra software. There are several on the market, but they may offer so much more that they will be just more confusing as well. So, unless you are already familiar enough with word-processing not to be confused, it will pay you to follow the four exercises offered here.

You may find them rudimentary because word-processors, being descendents of the iron age typewriter, all work on the same principles. Once you've mastered WordPad, a more sophisticated system will be much easier to manage.

To open the program **WordPad**, go ⁂ **start** – **All Programs** – **Accessories** and look for **WordPad**. Click that. On your screen is now a window called **Document – WordPad**, a blank page for you to type on.

Whatever your interest in computers, you will need the basic skills of word-processing, if only just to type the name of a File. Trial and error will teach you much, but follow the few tips given here.

The first essential is to get acquainted with the signs and symbols showing in the **Document – WordPad** window.

At the top of the window is the **Title-bar** with the name **Document – WordPad** appearing in light-coloured characters on a dark-coloured bar, as a title does in all windows. At the right-hand end of the title-bar are our friends the three little Buttons for maximizing, shrinking and closing.

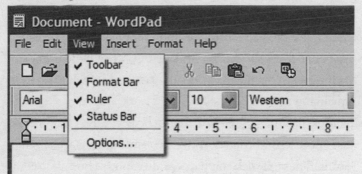

Below the Title-bar is the **Menu bar**. Menus vary from window to window. This one offers **File, Edit, View, Insert, Format** and **Help**. Click the word **File** and briefly cast your eye down the Menu which appears. Click **Edit** to glance at that Menu and then move over to **View**. On the View Menu are listed **Toolbar, Format Bar, Ruler** and **Status Bar,** each preceded by a **tick ✓** (or **check mark,** as the Americans call it). Note that Menu options are specific to the windows in which they appear.

Next below the Menu bar is *usually* the **Toolbar,** recognizable by its display of icons, one of which is 🖫 also known as **Save.** If the Toolbar isn't showing, click open the **View** menu and if **Toolbar** isn't ticked there, click on it. That will produce both a tick on the Menu and the appearance on screen of the Toolbar. If, on the **View** Menu, there is a ✓ opposite **Toolbar** and you click it, the tick will disappear from the Menu and the Toolbar will disappear from view. (This means you can see more of what you are typing.)

The Toolbar presents a row of icons. Icons come into their own here, because there is no room to display their names. These names you can see if you rest your ▷ over a Button. After a moment it will announce its function. Just for fun, click 📅 , the Button at the extreme right, the one which calls itself **Date/Time.** Choose a style from the varieties you're offered and click **OK.** The date will now appear in your document. Delete it by pressing the **backspace key,** the one with a left-pointing arrow ◄——— . If you put your ▷on the Toolbar in a space between icons, you can move it about by dragging.

The next line down is *usually* the **Format bar**. It can also be moved about by dragging. The oblong box on its left shows the name of the font (style of print or type face) currently operating. The box with a number in it refers to the size of print. The icon on the right, beginning with **B** for bold, also affects the form of what you type. Like all icons, those on the format bar can be pressed or released.

B becomes **B** when pressed once, and **B** when pressed again. This clicking and re-clicking is called **toggling**. Pass your ⃕ along this bar, slowly, so as to give the icons time to announce their functions.

The line below is *usually* the **ruler**, and this can also be turned on or off by ticking/unticking on the View Menu.

When you've finished with the WordPad window, click its ⊠. Then, when you're asked whether or not you want to save changes, click No.

EXERCISE 6

WORD-PROCESSING

6.ii Starting to Type

Start this exercise with WordPad. (**start** – All Programs
– Accessories – WordPad.)

Move your mouse all over the WordPad window which
appears. As you do, you'll see the **mouse pointer** Ⅰ . Move
it around with your mouse and you will see that it takes this
shape when in a part of the screen on which you can type,
but reverts to the second mark, your old friend the **mouse
arrow** ⬚ , when there is something to be pointed at, such
as an icon, or a Menu. Another mark you'll see is a blinking
vertical line called the **Cursor,** |. Once you begin typing, it
never stops blinking but waits for another character to be
typed. As you type, the characters land on the space
occupied by the Cursor, and the Cursor moves one space to
the right to make room for the next character.

Examine your keyboard and look for familiar-looking
typewriter keys. Some will be strange. Try them out to see

what they do. The group on the right of the keyboard with numbers on them is for doing sums. We'll come to that later. You can also ignore, for the moment, the F keys at the top. They are mostly a hangover form the days before the invention of the mouse, when everything was controlled from the keyboard. Almost everything can still be controlled from the keyboard, but the mouse, which began as a convenience, can still be a necessity.

Now type something, at least two paragraphs of it. Note that what you type appears where the Cursor is, not where the mouse pointer I happens to be. To **get the Cursor where you want it to be** (within the text you have typed), put the mouse pointer I at the chosen spot and click. The blinking Cursor will follow. You may find, until you get used to it, that you try to type where the pointer is, not where the Cursor is, because you've forgotten to move the Cursor to where you want to type.

To move the pointer across the page by large amounts, moving it by moving the mouse and clicking where you want to anchor it is fine, but for small jumps, such as between letters, you may find that the four **arrow keys on the keyboard** (←↓↑→) are easier to control.

The key **Home** jumps the Cursor to the beginning of a line, the key **End** jumps it to the end. If you hold down the key **Ctrl** (Control) at the same time as the **Home** or **End** keys, the Cursor goes to the beginning or end of the whole document. In order to produce capital letters, as well as the symbols such as ! @ £ % and so on which appear at the top of the number and symbol keys, press the **shift key** ⇧ at the same time as pressing the relevant key.

If you've typed an incorrect letter, press the **backspace** key. This deletes what's immediately to the left of the Cursor. The key called **Delete** deletes all sorts of things, but, when you're typing, it deletes what lies immediately to the right of the Cursor.

Unlike the behaviour of an iron age typewriter, when letters typed by a word-processor reach the end of a line they automatically go down to the line below, a process called **wordwrapping**. Pressing the **Enter** key interrupts this automatic process when you decide, for instance, to start a new paragraph. Pressing **Enter** puts you down at once to the start of the next line below. (To **reverse such an Enter**, press the backspace key.) If, at the beginning of a new paragraph, you want to start a few spaces in, first press the **Tab** key, the key with two opposite facing arrows on it ⇄, found just above the **Caps Lock** key at the left of the keyboard. It may be no longer fashionable to indent paragraphs, but many people prefer to do so.

The **Caps Lock** key controls whether you type in **UPPER CASE** (capitals) or lower case. Press it once to go on and once again to go off (toggling it on and off). It can be maddening when you forget **Caps Lock** is on, but on some keyboards there is a warning light (see on the keyboard top right), telling you that **Caps Lock** is operating. Not all word-processors are clever enough to change to lower case something you've already typed in upper case letters.

If you press the **Insert** key, and put the Cursor immediately to the left of a letter already typed, what you now type will replace that letter. This is unnerving when you've pressed **Insert** by mistake, especially as the space bar now acts like the **Delete** key, deleting what's to the right. Press the **Insert** key again to get out of trouble.

Note the **Page Up** and **Page Down** (Pg Up and Pg Dn) keys at the right of the keyboard. These can help you to move up and down a long document, rather than using the arrow keys (which are slower) or the mouse and scroll bar (which can be unreliable).

Finish this exercise by clicking the ⊠ in the top right-hand corner of screen. You will then be asked whether or not you want to save changes. Click **No**.

EXERCISE 6

WORD-PROCESSING

6.iii Highlighting

You need WordPad again for this exercise. (**start** – **All Programs** – **Accessories** – **WordPad**.) Type a few sentences so as to produce some text on which to practise.

If you want to alter the appearance of what you have typed you must first pick out the bit you want to change by highlighting it. Highlighting is also known as selecting. The word highlighted is highlighted, dark letters on a light background changed to light letters on a dark background.

There are several ways of doing this. One is by using the mouse pointer, $\rceil$. **To highlight a single word**, move the mouse pointer over it and double-click. To **highlight a chunk of text**, put the pointer at one end of it and hold down the clicker while dragging in any direction, sideways or up and down. You can achieve the same effect from the keyboard by keeping the shift key ⇧ pressed while moving the Cursor about with the arrow keys or pressing the **Home** or **End** keys. Rather than use the wobbly mouse pointer to **highlight a single letter**, you may prefer to use the keyboard: press at the same time the shift key and an arrow key, either ← or → according to whether the mouse pointer is on to the right or the left of the character, so as to highlight just that letter. Only one word or whole section can be highlighted in one go – there cannot be unhighlighted chunks of text between highlighted words or sections. **To highlight a whole document**, either put your mouse pointer at the top left of the page and drag it to bottom right, or choose **Select All** from the **Edit** Menu. To **remove highlighting**, one click anywhere other than the highlighted section will do this. To delete what it is that you've highlighted, press **Delete**.

If you want to underline what you have typed, highlight it and click the **U** icon on the format bar. What you have highlighted then becomes underlined. To remove underlining, highlight what's underlined, click the **U** icon again and then click anywhere else. By toggling on the **B** **I** **U** icons you can make type **bold**, put it in *italics*, underline it or revert to un-bold, un-italicized or un-underlined. You can have the **B** **I** **U** icons all pressed down *at the same time.*

Besides using the **Delete** key, you can also remove what you've highlighted by clicking the **scissors icon** ✂, seen up there in the Toolbar. Try this out. Highlight something and cut it out with the scissors. It vanishes, but hasn't gone forever, because up there, three icons to the right of the scissors icons on the Toolbar, is the "Whoops sorry" icon ↺. (If you rest your arrow on it and wait for half a second, you'll see that its name is **Undo**, short for **Undo Last Command**.) Click this and what you've just cut out will reappear. This is an icon to be blessed, because it's so easy to make a mistake.

To repeat, to remove highlighting, click anywhere. To delete what's highlighted, click ✂ or press the **Delete** key. Regretted actions are reversible by ↶ **Undo**.

Cut, Copy and Paste ✂ 📋 📋

Scissors do more than just cut out what's highlighted; they *remember* what has been cut. Having cut a single letter, a word, a sentence or a whole File, you can then paste 📋 what you've cut out anywhere you like, as many times as you like, and even into a different document, such as an e-mail letter or Address Book. To choose where you want it to be pasted, mark the place you want to put it (called the **insertion point**) by putting the Cursor there. Then click on **Paste** 📋 and the job's done.

If an item is *dimmed* out, that means there is nothing for it to do. **Paste**, for instance, on the **Edit** Menu or ✂ , the scissors icon on the Toolbar, only work if something has been highlighted to be pasted or to be cut.

Now rest your arrow on the icon 📋 between **Cut** and **Paste**. Its name, **Copy**, will soon appear. Highlight some text, click **Copy**, and nothing much seems to happen apart from the highlighting. Your machine has copied what you have just highlighted and will paste it wherever you choose an insertion point by putting the Cursor there and clicking 📋 **Paste**. Once something is copied, you can swan all around your computer before going to where you want to paste it. And, you can paste the same stuff over and over. But, beware, anything awaiting pasting will be replaced by anything that's cut or copied afterwards. The earlier version, if cut out without being copied, will be forgotten, lost for ever, because only one bit of highlighting can be memorized at a time.

By clicking on the **Edit** Menu or on the Toolbar Buttons, you can **Cut, Copy** and **Paste** from one document to another and from one part of a document to another part of the same document. You can also **drag text** from one part of a document to another part. Highlight a word or some text and click elsewhere and that will abolish the highlighting, but if you keep the mouse Button pressed you can drag what's highlighted to another position on the page. If you keep the **Ctrl** key pressed while doing this, the action won't just move what's highlighted but will leave the original intact where it was, making a copy of it elsewhere.

Mouse versus Keyboard

Apart from typing on the **keyboard** and using keys like **Delete**, shift and the arrow keys, many of the manoeuvres of this exercise have been done with the mouse alone. All of it, however, can be done direct from the keyboard, and, while you are engaged in typing, this may be more convenient than stopping to handle the mouse. Windows has many ways of doing the same thing and keyboard methods have survived alongside the introduction of mouse control.

If you highlighted something for underlining and absentmindedly pressed the **Delete** key, you could use the mouse to click ↶ , the **Undo** icon, and rescue it. But, you could also order **Undo** from the keyboard. By holding down the **Alt** key and then pressing **E** (**E** for **Edit**), the **Edit** Menu appears. You can select any of the options on this Menu by either clicking on it or using the arrows keys to move the highlighting up and down. An item on this Menu is **Undo Ctrl+Z**, meaning that pressing the keys **Ctrl** and **Z** together gives the same command as clicking the **Undo** icon (but you cannot do this while the Edit menu is opened up). The keyboard shortcut for **Cut** on the keyboard is **Ctrl+X**, as you will see on the drop down **Edit** Menu. **Copy**, on the keyboard is **Ctrl+C** and **Paste** is **Ctrl+V**. Do what suits you best, probably a combination of mouse and keyboard.

In many word-processing programs you can highlight a whole line by clicking at its extreme left, in the margin. This means that if you use the mouse pointer to get the Cursor to the beginning of a line, it's very easy to go too far and stray into the margin and click there. If you do that, you'll highlight the line. If you don't want to highlight a line but go to its beginning, it's better to send the Cursor there by pressing **Home**, rather than using the mouse pointer.

Finish this exercise by clicking the ⊠ in the top right-hand corner of the screen. You will then be asked whether or not you want to save changes. Click **No**.

EXERCISE 6

WORD-PROCESSING

6.iv Further Refinements

Once again, open WordPad. (**start** – All Programs – Accessories – WordPad.)

Changing Fonts
Type in the WordPad window the sentence 'The quick brown fox jumps over the lazy dog'. It will appear on your screen in the default font, probably one called **Times New Roman**.

To choose a different **font** for that sentence, first highlight it and then click the little arrow in the left box of the format bar. When you scroll to a font listed there and click it, the quick brown fox sentence will appear in that font. If you scroll to a font called **Arial**, click that. What then appears is **The quick brown fox jumps over the lazy dog**. Different computers have different fonts on them, but somewhere amongst your list of fonts you may find some which produce symbols in the place of letters. If you chose the font Webdings, you will see ▓▓▓ ()▓▓□✈ ▓✗▲▌● ▓▄⊘ ▄▓!▓? ▄▓▓✗ ▓▓▓ ✚✓⊗⊖ ♥▄■. The fourth group of symbols, ▓▄⊘, was produced by typing the letters f, o and x, so if you wanted to produce the symbol ▓, you'd choose Webdings as your font and type f on the keyboard. Thus, that sentence about the fox and the dog, famous for containing all the letters of the alphabet, comes in useful when wondering how to type a symbol like Webdings which has no obvious relation to the keyboard. If you haven't got Webdings try a symbol font you do have. You can choose a font before typing text or you can highlight text and then choose what font you want for it.

Changing Point Size

The size of type is measured in points, one point being one 72nd of an inch. To change **point** size, highlight what you want to change, say the character ▓. (You will remember that, to highlight a single character, you put the mouse pointer immediately to its right or to its left and, with the shift key ⇧ pressed, move over the character by using the arrow keys.) Now click the little down arrow ▾ in the box with a number in it. This number refers to point size. (The box is seen on the Tolbar between the font name box and **B** *I* **U** .) Scroll to a number, say 18, to choose a different point size. The character ▓ will now become larger. As with fonts, and as with **B** *I* **U** , you can choose what you want before typing text or you can highlight text and then change it.

Viewing Fonts

There are two ways:

1. **❙ start** – **Control Panel** – **Fonts**. Double-click on any font listed there and the whole range of characters in that font is displayed.

2. In the WordPad window, click the **Format** Menu and choose **Font…** You are now offered just a sample of each font (and also a choice of size.) Whatever you choose and confirm by clicking on **OK** will operate anew when you start typing or will change what you have highlighted.

Keep your wits about you when changing font size or type. A change can alter how much text will appear on a printed page. Some fonts take up less room than others.

Margins

To control **margins** on a whole page, choose **Page Setup** on the File Menu of the WordPad window. The margins are demonstrated on a small model of the page showing at the top of the **Page Setup** window.

Type in the required measurements in the relevant boxes as shown on the next page, not forgetting to click **OK**. (When **form-filling**, that is to say going from one box to another in a window, you can jump from box to box by pressing the **Tab** key.)

You may find that setting new margins, though showing on the ruler, has no effect on what you type. If so, you may be victim of the command **No wrap** or **Wrap to window**. These commands can be reversed by choosing **Options** on the **View** Menu and clicking the **Text** tab in the **Options** window. Choose **Wrap to ruler** (not forgetting the **OK**) and your new margins will now behave. Note that altering the margins of a document will also alter how the page appears when printed.

This is an example of a frustrating situation where one command has been overruled by another somewhere in the system. If the **Page Up, Page Down, Ctrl+Home** and the **Ctrl+End** keys don't work, it may be because a command window is open. A click anywhere is often the cure. If the wrong document appears, just ☒ it away; maybe some other

File is waiting to be saved. Another example: your typing refuses to start on the left of the page. Perhaps there is a tab on your ruler (see page 56) or perhaps **Alignment Right** ≣ has been selected. It often helps to go back to the Desktop or even start – shut down and switch on again.

First Aid When Stuck

1. Press the space bar once. Try a left-click. Try a right-click. Try **Esc** (escape), the top left-hand key on the keyboard, though it's never worked for me.

2. Repeat what you had been trying to do. You may have pressed the wrong key or clicked the wrong icon.

3. Look at your screen; there may be an instruction there, such as **press any key**, or there may be an unchecked **Yes, No, OK, Cancel, Done, Close, Quit, Display** or **Exit** or **Apply**.

4. Is an unwanted command operating? See if any icon is pressed in or highlighted on the Toolbar or format bar, such as **Align right** or **Center**.

5. Note that when you want to reverse an action, toggling may work rather than **Undo**. Note also that you can often get rid of something stuck on your screen by calling up something else.

6. Remember that Menus, such as **View** or **Edit**, refer only to the window in which they appear. Menus in a window that lists the *names* of Files, for instance, differ from those in a window which shows the *contents* of a particular File.

There are more remedies listed in the index under **stuck**.

Tabs

(The same word **'tabs'** as on page 24 but used here in a different sense.) You can alter the margins of a line or a paragraph by dragging the **blobs on the ruler**. The blob on the left has an upper and a lower part. The upper part controls the first line of a paragraph, the lower part the rest of the paragraph.

To set the tabs, click on the ruler where you want to set them. A mark like **L** will appear. You can drag a tab in either direction. It will operate when you press the Tab key ⇄. To get rid of tabs, drag them off the ruler, or click the **Format** Menu, choose **Tabs** and click **Clear All** and **OK**.

Find

This command is used for **finding a word in a document**. To practise this, type on the WordPad window a few lines of writing which contain the word **bath**. To find the word **bath**, click the find icon 🔍 (or something similar) on the Toolbar or click **Find** in the **Edit** Menu, so as to open the **Find** window. Accept the invitation of the blinking Cursor and type, in the **Find what:** box, the word **bath**. Then click **Find Next**. The word **bath** becomes highlighted, even if it's on page 100. Now ☒ away the **Find** window.

Here's another refinement. Add another word **Bath** to the document, this time spelt with a capital **B**. Click open the **Find** window. Click the ? and move the mouse to rest the ? on **Match case** and click.

The answer goes something like this:

> Finds only text with uppercase and lowercase characters as specified in **Find what**.

Click away the answer and click a tick against **Match case**. In the **Find what:** box delete the word **bath** and type **Bath** with a capital **B**. Now, when you click **Find Next**, the word **bath** won't be found but the word **Bath** will be.

You can also replace one word, wherever it occurs, with another. To try this, choose **Replace** on the **Edit** Menu and type in your desired replacement, say **Bristol**. Click **Replace All** and each word **Bath** in the document will be changed to the word **Bristol**. ✖ away the **Find** window and click anywhere to remove the highlighting.

Bullet Points

▤ the icon on the extreme right of the format bar, when clicked, starts a paragraph with a **bullet point** •. To cancel a bullet, don't try to **Delete** it but remember that toggling is the way to reverse the action of an icon. **Undo** won't pull the icon ▤ out, clicking the icon will.

Making a Letterhead

This can be done with a manoeuvre called **Scrap** (this works with WordPad, not on all word processors). You can make several scraps and drag them into a **Folder** (see page 64 for making a **Folder**) which can then act as a clipboard containing more than one item waiting to be copied, unlike the one-item-at-a time-only

and invisible **clipboard** which can be loaded by Cut or
Copy.

Highlight and Delete anything you've typed so as to clear
the page, and type a letterhead using the alignment, point
and font of your choice, say:

DR. BARKING-MADDE
THE DOGHOUSE
HOUNDSDITCH
BERKS

To change the **alignment** in WordPad, use the icons
towards the right of the Toolbar. To change to alignment
left press ≣; to change to centred alignment (as above) press
≣ , and to change to alignment right press ≣ .

You could also, if you have a colour printer, **highlight for
colour printing** any part of it and choose a colour from the
color icon 🎨 on the format bar.

Now reduce with 🗗 the size of the WordPad window so
as to reveal a bit of Desktop. Highlight what you have typed,
put the mouse pointer over the highlighting and drag what
you've highlighted onto the Desktop. An icon appears on
the Desktop labelled *WordPad Document Scrap 'Dr.
Barking-Ma…'*. Change that name to something simpler,
say Letterhead (see page 13 to remind you how to change
the name of an icon).

Letterhead remains on your Desktop ready for future
use, because, when you next open WordPad to write a letter,
you can reduce it so as to reveal the bit of Desktop which
shows Letterhead on it and drag Letterhead on to your

new letter. There, ready typed, will be your letterhead in whatever colours or style you had chosen.

You can have **today's date** typed in automatically by clicking **Date and Time** on the **Insert** Menu (or the **Date/Time** icon at the right end of the Toolbar 🔲) and OK-ing the style you want.

Finish this exercise by clicking the ⊠ in the top right-hand corner of the screen. Click **No** when you're asked whether or not you want to save changes.

EXERCISE 7

MAKING FILES AND FOLDERS

Saving

If you have any experience at all of word-processing, you will have learned, the hard way, that your work can disappear in a flash. Forever. This can happen if there's a power cut or if someone in the kitchen switches on a faulty gadget. The reason is that what you type is memorized only temporarily by your machine. If it's not permanently recorded – saved – before electricity is next cut off, it's gone.

People don't just go white after power cuts: they jump out of skyscraper windows. And then there's the **illegal operation**. Sometimes a window appears accusing me of having performed one. I am forced to click **Close** to shut that shameful window, but in doing so I lose any changes I have made since I last saved. This is particularly cruel because I have no notion of what I have done wrong.

One reason why beginners with Windows get confused is that there are so many ways of doing the same thing. Saving a document is a good example. You could click **File**, to reveal the Menu, and then click the **Save** which appears there and that would take the document out of temporary memory. Or you could, as suggested on that Menu, press **Ctrl+S** on your keyboard. Or, yet another way, you could click the third icon from the left along the Toolbar, 🖫 , which is also **Save**. I myself prefer to open the **File** Menu with my mouse and click on **Save**, rather than click on the 🖫 icon, simply because the icon is a bit insignificant for me to aim at.

When should you save? Being twice-shy I do it several times a page, any time I leave the room, and whenever I feel I owe it to posterity to preserve some thought of genius. This may be unnecessary; your machine will remind you at every opportunity not to forget to save. But I am terrified of the accusation of illegal operations and my electricity comes along wires supported by ancient wooden poles. Some word-processing **software** can save Files automatically, at chosen intervals.

It is still possible to lose stuff even if power cuts and illegal operations are avoided. We've seen that if you cut out some text and copy another lot before pasting it in, the first lot is lost to limbo. Another hazard is that a text window, opened as usual by double-clicking its icon+name, may, for no apparent reason, suddenly close back to the icon+name, losing everything on it. "The best-laid schemes o'mice an' men gang aft a-gley", especially o'mice.

Save As
If you have just typed a document – made a File – and clicked its ⊠ , your caring machine will want to make sure

you really want to lose it, and so you will be asked **Save
changes to document? Yes, No** or **Cancel**. Click **No** and
it will disappear, but if you want to save it, what do you do?
Let's type a new document and find out.

Open WordPad (**start** – **All Programs** – **Accessories**
– **WordPad**.) and type **Summer, sea, sand and sun**. This
is a five-word File. In computer-speak, a File consists of **data**,
plural of the Latin word datum. If these data are not to be
lost, they must be saved. Drop down the **File** Menu and click
the **Save As** bar (or click the 💾 icon or save it some other
way).

You'll now see, blinking, a request for a **File name**. (If
there's nothing blinking, get the Cursor into the **File name**
box, if necessary clearing out, by means of the backspace
key, anything already there. Type in a name for your
document, say **Bermuda**. Near where you typed **Bermuda**
there's a Button called **Save**. Don't click it yet, because

you've still to decide *where* to store your document. Decide this by selecting something from the choice presented by clicking the ☑ icon in the **Save in** box. Click 🖴 **(C:)**. That action decides that your File will be stored in the huge filing cabinet called **C** (introduced in the next exercise). Having chosen a name and a place, you can now click **Save**.

Your document reappears, its name now changed from **Document – WordPad**, to **Bermuda – WordPad**, safe!

You *could* now remove it from the screen by ❎ing WordPad to get back to the Desktop before starting on your second document, but you don't *have* to clear the screen before opening another window. Go again to ⧉ **start** – **All Programs – Accessories – WordPad** and when you click **WordPad, Bermuda** just gets covered up behind the new **Document – WordPad** window. (The most recently opened window is always in front.) In your new window, type the words **Winter, ski, snow and sun.** Click the **File** Menu and choose **Save as** (or click the save icon). In the **Save as** window, select 🖴 **(C:)** again for the **Save in** box, and type **Austria** in the **File name** box. Now that you've chosen a name for your File and a place to store it in, click the **Save** icon. Your document reappears in the WordPad window, now entitled – **Austria – WordPad**, safe! Click its ❎ to reveal the File **Bermuda** lurking behind it. Click **Bermuda's** ❎ and you're back to the Desktop.

Now let's check that your two Files are safely stored in **C**. Double-click **My Computer**. The **My Computer** window has a left and a right **pane**, with a toolbar above. Clicking the 📁 **Folders** button on the toolbar toggles the left pane between a list of useful tasks, places and details, and a list

called **Folders**. Try it. The right pane shows what's inside
any folder you click in the left pane. Click Local Disk (C:)
on the left and, sure enough, there in the right pane
Bermuda and Austria are listed. (You may have to scroll
to the right to see where they are.)

Let's make a Folder called Holidays and put the Files
Austria and Bermuda into it. Our C window is open, and
that's the filing cabinet where we want to store this Folder.
Right-click any empty space in this window and choose
New from the Menu that appears and then Folder. A
yellow Folder appears:

Type Holidays in the blinking name space and click (or
press the Enter key) to confirm.

To put the File Bermuda in this Holidays Folder, drag
it towards the Folder until Holidays becomes highlighted.
Then release the clicker and the job's done. Do the same
with Austria. You can leave that C window open while
going to start for the third File we propose to create.

For this, go start – All Programs – Accessories
and, instead of WordPad, this time click Paint. Study this
window. Have a look at what the Buttons on the left of the
Paint window do by resting your arrow on them one by one.
(These Buttons make up the Toolbox. This behaves like the
Toolbar in that, if it's not showing, a click against Toolbox
in the View Menu to tick it will make it show.) Click Pencil
(though the Pencil Button 🖉 is probably already pressed
down by default). Move the arrow to the blank page and

you'll find you can click and drag the pencil about to make a drawing. (If nothing happens, try a right-click.) Try and draw a palm tree. If you get into a muddle and want to start again, click the **Image** Menu and click **Clear Image**. If you can't manage a palm tree, just make any old squiggle. (To avoid complications, please postpone having fun with this program until after this exercise. To find **Paint** again, all you need is **start** – All Programs – Accessories – Paint.)

Note that your drawing, just pencilled lines, can also be known as a File or document, and that it consists of data. It must now be named and saved, so click **File – Save As**. This time we'll **save it into the Holidays Folder**. To do this, click the scroll Button ⚫ in the **Save in** box and choose **C** from the list. Then click the **Holidays** Folder which appears below. Click **Open**, and the **Holidays** Folder appears in the **Save in** box, opened in readiness to receive the drawing you are about to name. In the **File name** box, type in the name **Coconut**. Click **Save**. The drawing is now named **Coconut** and is saved in the **Holidays** Folder in the cabinet called **C**. It reappears, now entitled **Coconut-Paint**, safe! ❌ it away to return to the **C** window. Click open the **Holidays** Folder and there a drawing called **Coconut** is listed along with **Bermuda** and **Austria**. Close the **Holidays** Folder.

Lists and Details

With the **C** window open in My Computer, the ▦ button on the toolbar offers you different ways of showing, in the right-hand pane, those Files and Folders within the cupboard called **C**, most of which are of no interest. **Tiles** and **Icons** look pretty similar, while **List** is just that. **Details** gives – surprise, surprise – details about the items. **Thumbnails** is handy if you're looking for pictures or photographs (but better still, look out for **Filmstrip**, offered when you're searching through a folder full of pictures).

Let's pick the **Details** view. Clicking on *Name, Size, Type* and *Date Modified* along the top of the right-hand pane, changes the order in which things are listed. For instance, *Name* put everything in alphabetical order – Folders first, then Files; click on *Size* and you'll see that even a simple picture File is much bigger than a plain text File. Exactly the same Views choices are listed in the **View** Menu, as are the listing options (click **Arrange icons by**).

Making New Folders

We made a new Folder, Holidays in the ⬚ (C:) window. You can put a new Folder on the Desktop or in any window which can provide storage for it. Right-click over this potential storage place and you will be offered a Menu containing the item **New**. Click that and then click **Folder**. ⬚ New Folder appears.

Give it a name and remember where you put it. You can open a new Folder in a Folder window like **Holidays**, because a Folder is a storage place which can itself contain a new Folder – a sub-Folder if you like to call it that. But, if you right-click in a window like WordPad or Solitaire, you'll get different instructions or no instructions, because, though you can put a File into a Folder, you can't put a Folder into a File or a program.

When you are saving a File into a folder, the **Save**

Button on the **Save as** window may say **Open**, not **Save**. That means that a Folder is showing in the window as a possible storage space. Clicking that **Open** Button opens the Folder ready for accepting the File you are saving.

Go back to the Desktop ready for Exercise 8.

EXERCISE 8

DRIVES C AND A

The correct computer-speak name for **C**, the cupboard in which we stored our holiday documents, is **Hard disk drive C**. For us beginners, however, it helps to think of it as a *place* where you can store information. Ignore the differences between **C**, **[C]**, **local disk [C:]** and **C:** which you may see on various windows; they all refer to the same place.

With a double-click, open **C** in the **My Computer** window and there you will see the **Holidays** Folder you put there. Open that Folder with a double-click and there are your three Files, listed in the order you selected from **Arrange Icons** in the **View** Menu.

The computer-speak name for **A** (also known as **drive A**, **[A]**, **A:**, or **A:** is **3½ Floppy [A:]**. Its main purpose is to copy Files and Folders on to **Floppy disks**. It can also let you see the contents of floppy disks made by other people.

You can make as many copies of a floppy disk as you wish, then you can send them by post or store them in the bank or in a fireproof safe. Once your stuff is saved onto floppies, you aren't completely ruined if your computer is struck by lightning or stolen by burglars. But, like everything in this ever-changing world, they don't last forever. They hate dust, coffee, gin-and-tonic and even water; but, above all, they hate magnets. Cordless phones and loudspeakers contain magnets, so keep floppy disks away from them. (Loudspeakers supplied by computer dealers are shielded so as not to damage floppies.) Write a name on every floppy you use as one floppy may otherwise by indistinguishable from another.

The common size is 1.44 MB. MB stands for **megabyte**, a **byte** being the unit of measurement a computer uses to construct things like words. Files that show pictures are very greedy for bytes, but words are not. Just look at the **Details** (clickable on the **View** Menu of the **Holidays** window) of your **Coconut** File. My one took up 218kB compared with 5kB used by **Bermuda** and **Austria**. It is because films and music are such gigantic swallowers of bytes that they need special discs (CDs and DVDs) in order to be played on PCs.

Inserting a Floppy Disk

A floppy disk won't fit anywhere else in your machine other than in the floppy disk slot, and if it's the wrong way up it won't go in. Always hold a floppy by its labelled end. If it hasn't got a label, insert the disk with the metallic end first. The disk should be inserted with the round metallic shape facing downwards.

To see what's contained in a floppy disk sitting in its slot, double-click **My Computer** on the Desktop and then double-click **3½ Floppy [A:]** in the My Computer window

under the heading **Devices with Removable Storage**. If
there are any Files or Folders in that **A** cupboard, they will
be listed there.

A floppy disk must be **formatted** the first time it is used.
Formatting is an initiation ceremony to prepare a floppy for
being used in a computer. To format a floppy disk, put it into
the floppy disk slot. Double-click **My Computer** on the
Desktop. Then right-click the **3½ Floppy Disk** icon. Click
the **Start** Button in the window (not the ⊞ start Button
on the taskbar). A warning box may appear to which you
can click **OK**. If the disk you put into the slot was a
previously formatted disk with data on it, that data will be
wiped out during this reformatting, so don't pick up the
wrong one by mistake. A bright green bar moves across the
Formatting window until the job is done. If it tells you that
the format is complete, click **OK** and close the **Format**
window.

Before taking a floppy out of its slot, close the **3½
Floppy [A:]** window. Give your machine a moment or two
to realize it's gone before putting in another one.

Floppies are not capacious enough to contain more than
a few pages of material like this book, which has many
pictures, each requiring thousands of bytes. Fortunately,
there are disks available (such as **zip disks**) with capacities
like 100 megabytes and more, but to use them you need a
special slot and drive. I bless the day I had one installed.

EXERCISE 9

MOVING AND COPYING
FILES OR FOLDERS

Moving by Cut, Copy and Paste
Just as you can manipulate whatever it is that you have
highlighted – a character, a word or a chunk of text – by
using **Cut**, **Copy** or **Paste** from the **Edit** Menu (or by
clicking ✂ , 📋 or 📋 on the Toolbar), you can do the same
with a File or Folder in the My Computer window. You can
cut, copy or paste the whole contents of a File by
highlighting all of it with **Select All** from the **Edit** Menu,
but you can also cut or copy and paste a File or Folder by
highlighting just its *name*. You can move a File or Folder
from place to place or copy it elsewhere by dragging it.

Moving by Dragging
We dragged a bit of highlighted text to the Desktop to make
a readily available letterhead. As long as you can display a
bit of window and a bit of Desktop on the same screen you
can **drag** from one to the other; not just bits of text, but the

contents of Files or Folders. If you display two windows, or just enough of them, on the same screen, you can drag text, Files or Folders from one to the other. You can also drag an item to a temporary resting place in a corner of the Desktop, open a shrunken window for its destination, and then drag it there from the Desktop.

Dragging to a Floppy Disk

By copying stuff onto a floppy disk you can give it wings to fly away from your desk-bound machine. You can then send it to someone by post or make a backup copy of something as insurance against damage to the original. As an example of dragging to a floppy, open the **Holidays** Folder in **C** to show the name **Austria**, and, by manipulating the window – shrinking it with 🗗, or using the double-headed arrow ↕ or ⇖ in its title-bar to drag it out of the way – get 3½ **Floppy [A]** showing in the **My Computer** window as well. Provided there is a floppy in the slot waiting to receive it, drag **Austria** towards 3½ **Floppy [A]**. As you get near, 3½ **Floppy [A]** becomes highlighted. (That's how you know you are on target.) Release your clicker and you'll see **Austria** flying from **C** to **A**!

Moving Files to a Floppy Disk by **Send To**

This is by far the slickest way of making a backup copy of a File or Folder on a floppy. First, put a formatted floppy disk into the floppy disk slot to receive what you propose to **Send To** it. Then, open a window to expose the name of the item you want to make a backup of, say the **C** window which contains your **Holidays** Folder. Right-click on

Holidays, choose **Send To** and click 3½ **Floppy [A].** You can now watch the contents of the Folder **Holidays** flying over to the floppy disk. To see it there you'll have to get back to 3½ **Floppy [A]** on the **My Computer** window and double-click it open. You'll see there the **Austria** File you dragged there and the **Holidays** Folder you have just performed **Send To** on. Don't forget to label the floppy. When going from **C** to **A** this way, you don't just move something, you make a copy of it in **A** and leave the original behind in **C.**

Copying

The rule is that if you move something from one part of **C** to another part of **C,** or from one part of **A** to another part of **A,** you are just moving it; but, if you move something from **C to A by dragging** or by using **Send To,** you don't just move it, you make a copy of it in **A** and leave the original behind in **C.** You can break this rule for **Send To** by holding down shift when you click **Send To,** which means you don't leave a copy behind in **C.** You can also break it if, when dragging, you use the *right* mouse clicker and not the *left* one. If you use the right clicker for dragging, when you release it you're given, among the choices, **Move Here,** or **Copy Here.** Click your pick with the left mouse Button. Decide carefully. It's unwise to leave unnecessary copies strewn about, because the time will come when, after an alteration to a copy or its original, you won't know which is which. It's therefore worth cultivating the habit of always using the right clicker for moving Files and Folders and making a careful choice between **Move Here** and **Copy**

Here. Don't forget, either, that if you alter an original document in **C** after it's been copied to **A**, the copy in **A** remains unaltered unless recopied. But it's only a second's work to click the document's name, click the **File** Menu, **Send To 3½ Floppy [A]** and click **Yes** to the question **Would you like to replace the existing File with this one?**

Disk Space Available

When you have more than a few small Files to copy onto a floppy, an attempt at copying may be interrupted by the message **The disk in the destination drive is full**. To see what space is available on a floppy disk, go to **My Computer – 3½ Floppy [A]** (a single-click) – **File – Properties**. That shows you a **pie chart** with the answer. It's surprising how much space Paint Files occupy. (To see what space is available in **C**, go **My Computer – C** (single-click) – **File – Properties**.)

Copying files onto a CD or DVD

See Exercise 18, on page 99, for how to copy files to a CD.

To Recap…

COMPUTERS ARE KNOWN TO CRASH – KEEP BACKUP COPIES OF IMPORTANT STUFF ON FLOPPIES, CDs OR ANYWHERE OTHER THAN YOUR HARD DISK.

To make a back up, use **Send To** on the File Menu. Choose **3½ Floppy [A]** and click **Yes** to the question **Would you like to replace the existing File with this one?** if you want to update a copy already on a floppy.

EXERCISE 10

FINDING, DELETING AND RESTORING FILES AND FOLDERS

To Find a File or Folder

So far you've made only three Files, so it's easy to find any of them again, but say you had hundreds? No problem. If you remember where you saved a File you know where to look for it. You saved the File **Coconut** in the **Holidays** Folder, stored in the filing cabinet **C**. You could therefore find it by going **My Computer –** ➤ **(C:) – Holidays** and opening that. The **path** started from **C** and ended with the name of the File. This is the logical route, but not always the most practical, because many shortcuts are available.

One is the **Find** system from the ⊞ **start** Menu. (Do not confuse this with **Find** on the **Edit** Menu, which you used to find the word bath.) To find a File, go ⊞ **start**, up to Search, on the right and click. You now have a window called **Search Results**. In the blue pane on the left, you're asked **What do you want to search for?** The options available are mostly self-explanatory but you should click on **All Files**

and Folders. Next, under **Search by any or all of the criteria below,** you'll see some empty boxes and options to pick. In the first box, containing the blinking Cursor, type **Coconut,** or **cOconUt** but not **Cocoanut.** Case sensitivity doesn't matter, spelling does. Then click the ☑ Button in the **Look in** box to decide whether to look in **C** or **A.** Decide for the moment to look in **C.** Click **Search** and your **Coconut** File appears on the right. You'd be told that it is stored in **C:\Holidays,** and is 218 kilobytes (or something like that) in size. If you had chosen not **C** but **A,** provided the floppy was in its slot you'd see two Files called **Coconut** showing up, the one you dragged to **A** and the other contained in the **Holidays** Folder you **Sent To A.** If you had chosen **My Computer** in the **Look in** box, you'd find all three **Coconut Files** showing there, the one in **C** and the two in **A.** When maximized, the **Search Results** window will have room to give you the date and even the time when the various **Coconut** Files were last saved. You can open a File found in the **Search Results** window by double-clicking on its name.

You can also find a program in the **Search Results** window. Try and find Paint that way. But what if you don't remember the name you gave to a File, say to that palm tree drawing, and have even forgotten that you have a Folder called **Holidays?** There are several solutions.

1. Open a window, say **C,** showing the names of Files which might include the palm tree drawing. Then open the **View** Menu and select **Arrange Icons By – Name.** This puts the items in alphabetical order and might

remind you of its name. Among the dozens listed there Coconut shows up.

2. If that doesn't help, try **Arrange Icons By – Type**. This would immediately show up any picture File because all are grouped together.

3. **Arrange Icons By – Size** might be helpful, and so might **Modified**, if you had an idea when you last had the drawing of the palm tree on view.

4. In the **Search Results** window (under **All Files and Folders**) the search criteria can include all sorts of possible locations and options, which you can select to narrow your search.

5. Selecting options from **When was it modified?** can narrow down a search by specifying the date a File was last changed.

6. Searching for **A word or phrase in the file** shows you the results of every file containing that word or phrase in its text, not just its name.

Once a File or Folder's name appears in the **Search Results** window, you can double-click it open, or drag it elsewhere. Other ways of finding a File are mentioned in Exercise 11, on page 81.

Renaming a File or Folder

To rename a File or Folder you must find its name in a window (the **Search Results** window will do). If you wanted to change the name **Bermuda** in the **Holidays Folder** window, you first have to click **Bermuda** to highlight it and then give the name a second click (or press the **F2** key) to make the name blink. (If the second click followed too soon after the first one, the machine would interpret this as a double-click and open the File, but that's not what you want.) In the blinking name box, type a new name, say **Barbados**, followed by an **extension** that describes its type, in this case **.doc**. That is the extension which shows that it had its origin in WordPad. The three letters of an extension must be preceded immediately by a full stop. If you changed **Bermuda.doc** to **Barbados. doc**, you'd be in trouble because you'd put a space between the full stop and the **doc**. Confirm your new name by pressing **Enter** on the keyboard or by clicking elsewhere.

A name can be as long as 255 characters but can't include any of the characters \/:*? " < >. If, when trying to rename a File, you are presented with a warning like **Error Renaming File or Folder** this usually means that the File is already opened. If open, it will have its Button on the taskbar, so right-click the Button and click **Close**.

Deleting a File or Folder
To do this you must first find its name and highlight it. As happened with renaming a File, access will be denied if the File is currently open. If so, close it. When the name is highlighted, click **Delete** on the **File** Menu, or the delete icon on the Toolbar, or press the **Delete** key on the keyboard. The **Delete** key works anywhere, deleting anything that's highlighted: an icon on the Desktop, a File listed in a window or a piece of highlighted text.

Deletion transfers a File to a transit camp called the **Recycle Bin**. (It **deletes permanently** only if you press

Delete + Shift.) To see the Recycle Bin working, open your **Holidays** Folder via **My Computer – C – Holidays**, then highlight and Delete all three Files there, one by one. As you delete, you'll be asked to confirm this intention. Shut any windows hiding the Recycle Bin on your Desktop (or reveal the Desktop by clicking the 🗔 Button on your taskbar, if you have one there) and double-click **Recycle Bin** to open it. Your three Files are there.

If the same File exists in different places – a copy in **A**, for instance, and the original in **C** – deleting it in one place won't delete it in another. Your machine only does what it's told; it can't read your thoughts.

If the **Recycle Bin** icon is visible on the Desktop, you can drag things onto it there rather than highlighting and deleting them. To find a File in a crowded Recycle Bin don't forget its **View** Menu, which offers **Arrange Icons By.**

Unlike documents in **C**, which, when deleted, go to the Recycle Bin, an **item deleted from A** doesn't have that safeguard and disappears at one go. Beware! Even an immediate **Undo last command** won't rescue it.

Restoring a Deleted File

Highlight the File to be restored in the Recycle Bin window and click **Restore** on the **File** Menu. You can also drag a File out of the Bin into a window or onto the Desktop.

Permanent Removal from the Recycle Bin

To get rid of a File or Folder from the Recycle Bin, highlight it and press the **Delete** key. To empty the Recycle Bin at one go, open its **File** Menu and click **Empty Recycle Bin**.

Prune your Recycle Bin of rubbish whenever you have the courage. It occupies valuable space.

If you delete a Folder, it may sometimes appear in the Recycle Bin not as a Folder but as a list of all the Files it contains. To restore each one separately may be tedious but you can deal in **groups of Files**. This is looking forward to the day when you have lots of them. To handle more than one File at a time, click one to highlight it. With the Shift key pressed, click another File, separated from the first one by others. This will highlight not just the two Files you've clicked but all the Files between as well. To make an assorted bunch of Files you want to handle into a group, hold down the Ctrl key each time you highlight a File and they will all remain highlighted and can be dealt with as a bunch.

You can handle, in either of these two ways, groups of Files for deleting, copying or moving in other areas too. You can use the **Select All** Menu item in Edit to select all the Files in one Folder.

EXERCISE 11

SHORTCUTS

You could find the File **Coconut** by looking for it where you saved it, which was in the **Holidays** Folder you made in the C window. You could therefore reach it by going to **Desktop** – **My Computer** – ⬛ (C:) and clicking 📁 **Holidays**. But because you have recently worked on it, a quicker way is available. This is to go **start** and up the right-hand column to **My Recent Documents**, because this automatically lists the fifteen Files you have most recently worked on.

Look at **My Recent Documents** and there will be the names of the three Files you have made so far. You can single-click one to open it, just as you can single-click to select any item on any Menu.

To get a File listed in **My Recent Documents**, just opening it is enough, because a moment of attention is all that's required to qualify an item for inclusion as a recently worked document.

Making a Shortcut from the Desktop to a File or Folder

You could drag a File or Folder from any window onto a bit of Desktop, from where it could be opened by double-clicking. At first sight, this is a useful shortcut. But that File or Folder would be moved outright onto the Desktop, leaving nothing behind. From the Desktop it might even get sent by accident to the Recycle in, only to be permanently deleted when the Recycle Bin was next emptied. But if you used the right-clicker for dragging, you could choose Copy Here, so that the original would stay where it was and only a duplicate version planted on the Desktop. Dragging with the right clicker offers:

You might feel that copying was playing safe, by making an extra backup but, as you have been warned, scattering copies about can lead to confusion. Keep backups on CDs and floppy disks kept for that purpose.

It is better to make the other choice given to you when you right-click for dragging, **Create Shortcuts Here**. Try this, by dragging the name of the File Coconut onto your Desktop with your right clicker and choosing **Create Shortcuts Here**. This leaves the original safely where it was and puts just an icon on the Desktop, which you will see is labelled Shortcut to Coconut and maybe has a little shortcut arrow symbol in its corner. Double-clicking it opens the drawing, but deleting it deletes only the shortcut, not the drawing itself.

Shortcut from Desktop to your 3½ Floppy [A:]
Creating too many shortcuts on your Desktop may clutter it, but this one you may find useful. Go Desktop – **My Computer**– and, with the right clicker, drag **3½ Floppy [A:]** onto the Desktop. Click **Create Shortcuts Here**. A double-click on it there will open it.

Shortcut from One Folder to Another Folder or File
You can park a shortcut to a File or Folder temporarily on Desktop and drag it from the Desktop onto any window. You can then go direct from that window to the item you've made a shortcut to. Or you can create a shortcut to an item in any window by dragging that item's name onto the window with a right-click drag and choosing **Create Shortcuts Here**. This technique would be useful if you had a Folder containing many other Folders, each containing various chapters of a book, one of which you constantly referred to. You could drag the chapter on which you were working onto its mother Folder and create a shortcut to it there.

Shortcut from the Start Menu to a Program
Items on the **Start Menu** are shortcuts already. The "longcut" for instance, to Solitaire, is Desktop – **My Computer** – 🖴 (C:) – 📁 **Documents and Settings** – 📁 **All Users** – 📁 **Start Menu** – 📁 **Programs** – 📁 **Games** – **Solitaire**.

(There's even a shortcut from ⊞ start to 📁 **Programs** in the **Start Menu** window. It goes: right-click on ⊞ start – **Open**.) As an example, you could drag the program Solitaire or the program Calculator onto your Desktop to make a shortcut from there. You could also drag and drop a program like Calculator onto the ⊞ start Button. Then, when you clicked ⊞ start , **Calculator** would show in the left-hand column of the Menu and not on the far right. But, the simplest way to add a program to the **Start Menu** is to right-click on its icon. Click **Pin to Start Menu** and it's there. To remove it, right-click on its icon in the **Start Menu** and click **Unpin from Start Menu**.

Desktop Icons Misbehaving?
Right-clicking on your Desktop will give you a Menu for controlling the positions of the icons there. If, for instance, when you try to drag icons about the Desktop, they won't budge, you may be under the influence of Auto Arrange. Right-click on the Desktop and click **Arrange Icons by – Auto Arrange** so as to remove the tick mark ✓ alongside it and the icons will then obey your will. You can tidy up icons there, and make more desk space available, by making a new Folder on the Desktop and dragging them inside. (To remind you: right-click on the Desktop and select **New – Folder**. Type in a name and press **Enter** to confirm.)

EXERCISE 12

WINDOWS EXPLORER

In the last exercise we opened Folder after Folder, each containing other Folders. Starting from Desktop, we went My Computer – 🖴 (C:) – 📁 Documents and Settings – 📁 All Users – 📁 Start Menu – 📁 Programs – 📁 Games. Do this again, starting from Desktop and finishing up with 📁 Games. By pressing the **backspace** key ⬅—— , you can now retrace your steps. In this way you can go backwards from 📁 Games to My Computer, passing on the way 📁 Programs and 📁 Start Menu, 📁 All Users, 📁 Documents and Settings and 🖴 (C:). My Computer was the starting point for getting from the top of the mountainous pile of stuff in your computer down to Solitaire at the bottom.

You don't have to start from My Computer to view the whole shebang. There's another starting point for seeing what's in the valley below. This is Windows Explorer. This you find on the Accessories Menu in the All Programs Menu offered by the ⊞ start Button. Alternatively, right-click the **Start** Button and choose **Explore**. In **Windows Explorer** you are given a comprehensive view of the whole contents of your computer.

This window has two **panes**, one on the left and one on the right. (You can drag the dividing line between them to right or left with the double-headed arrow ◄──► which appears if you put your ↳ on the dividing line.) Make sure the left pane is scrolled to its top, either by dragging its slider upwards or clicking on the ▲ Button at the top of the scroll bar. Click an item in the left pane – [C:] or the **Recycle Bin**, or a Folder such as **Windows** – and its contents will show up in the right pane. When clicked, a Folder icon 📁 in the left pane will be seen to open, now 📂, its contents now showing up in the right pane. To close the Folder, click something else in the left pane – the right pane can display only one choice at a time.

In the left-hand pane you will see **plus signs** ⊞ . These are signs which say "There's a lot more inside". Click the ⊞ adjoining an item and it will show its subdivisions and change to ⊟. (Click the **minus sign** ⊟ to reverse this process.)

Lists and Details

Since the right-hand pane of the Explorer window gives you lists of Files and Folders, you can open the **View** Menu and click a view option. Also on that Menu is **Arrange Icons**. You will remember that if you choose **By Name** you will see that **Arrange Icons By Name** is computer-speak for **First list in numerical order Folders with names beginning with a number and follow this with a list, in**

alphabetical order, of those whose names begin with a letter; then do the same with Files. This numerical and alphabetical arrangement can make it easy to find what you want. Having gone down the mountain from left to right on Explorer you can go back up, Folder by Folder, by using the **backspace key** ◀────— .

Sorting Files and Folders

In the Explorer window, as with other windows and on the Desktop, you can drag Files in and out of Folders, and you can drag one Folder into another. If you reduce the size of the window so as to reveal some Desktop, you can drag a File onto the Desktop and move it again later into any old window. You can drag from A to C or from C to A, but this change to or from a floppy disk is a copying action unless you hold Shift down as you drag.

Don't be daunted by the apparent complexity of Windows Explorer. The Explorer window only looks complicated because there's so much in it. Much of the complexity of the **My Computer** method or the Windows Explorer method of listing Files and Folders can be avoided by **saving Files directly onto the Desktop**.

Until you have vast amounts of Files and Folders to cope with, when you have a new File and want to save it somewhere, you can click, when the **Save As** window comes up, **Desktop** in the **Save in** box. Give the new File a name in the **File Name** box, click **Save**, and it will then appear on your Desktop, instantly available just by double-clicking it there. If there are lots of such Files, personal letters for instance, make a right-click on your Desktop and make a new Folder, name it **Personal Letters** and drag the letters already on Desktop into it. A new letter can also go straight into that same Folder when you first save it. To do this, click Desktop in the **Save As** window, double-click the Folder listed there called **Personal Letters**, type a name for the letter in the **File Name** box, click **Save** and the letter will be stored as an item in the Personal Letters Folder on your Desktop.

EXERCISE 13

HELP

An extensive new **Help** and support program is found on the ⊞ **start** Menu. **Help** *specific* to a particular program is found as a Menu in the Menu bar of the window of that program. **Help** in the Solitaire window helps Solitaire; **Help** on the Paint window helps Paint. **Help** Menus offer tabs such as **Contents**, **Index** and **Search**.

Contents
There's useful stuff hidden in this section, but there are easier ways of looking at it.

Index
Index in the *general* **Help** program produces a vast list of subjects, most of which will never concern you. To get help, type in the box where the Cursor is blinking the first few letters of a title recognized by the machine. Type **bin** and you get nowhere, because those three letters are not the first letters of a recognized title, but type **recycle** or even just

recyc, and **Recycle Bin** will be highlighted. More choices are offered below the main entry. Choose **Emptying** and then click **Display** to see how to do this – as if you didn't know already!

Search

Search looks for a word that figures in the title of a subject. Type the word **recycle,** click the arrow and, because **recycle** is part of a known title, you're given choices – one of which is **Empty the Recycle Bin.** Click on this and instructions appear in the panel on the right. To look for something else, type in the new word.

Right-Clicking for Help

Sometimes a right-click over something produces a **What's this?** question, which, when clicked, gives an answer. Try this on the buttons in the Calculator window. (**start** – **All Programs – Accessories – Calculator.**)

EXERCISE 14

CLOCK AND DATE

If the digital **clock** is not showing on your taskbar, right-click **start** – **Properties** – **Taskbar** and tick ✓ **Show the Clock**.

Today's date can be seen if you rest your mouse arrow on the clock showing on the right of the taskbar and wait.

To adjust the time or the date, open the **Date and Time Properties** window by double-clicking the clock on the taskbar. Click the **Date & Time** tab, if it's not already showing, and make the necessary changes in the white boxes.

Your computer has been programmed automatically to take care of the changeover between **Summer and Winter time**. You can satisfy yourself that this is so by opening the **Date and Time Properties** window and clicking the **Time Zone** tab. You'll see that **Automatically adjust clock for daylight saving changes** is ticked and you'll be agreeably surprised to see, come Spring and Autumn, a message on your screen confirming that this has been done.

EXERCISE 15

CHARMAP

Charmap is short for character map. It provides characters which aren't available on the keyboard. If you intend to type in **French or other languages,** invest in an appropriate keyboard or software, because it can be tedious to rely on the Charmap for typing words like tété à tété or señorita. But Charmap is good for the occasional use. Find it by going ![start] – **All Programs** – **Accessories** – **System Tools.**

Once in a document, open the Character Map window and point your mouse ⬚ on the character you want and click. Then click **Select** and then **Copy.** The character – or characters – is/are now stored on your invisible clipboard, waiting to be pasted when you switch back to the document on which you're working. Choose an insertion point and click **Paste.**

Note the name in the **Font box** in the Charmap window. Different fonts give you a different set of characters. Have a look at what they offer you. If, when you paste, the **Charmap character differs from what you expected,** the font you copied it from is not the same as the one you are pasting into. Once you have pasted in the new character, highlight it and change the font from the font box on the Toolbar.

Note also the **Keystroke** box in the bottom right-hand corner of a Charmap. The keystroke, for instance, for the è in très bien is **Alt + 0232**. To use it, keep **Alt** pressed while you press the number on the keys on the right of your keyboard. When you release Alt, the **keystroke character from Charmap** appears. As the ½ of **3½ Floppy** recurs in this book, I have jotted down the keystroke **Alt+0189**. For this technique to work, the **Num Lock** key must be pressed so that its light is lit up on the keyboard.

Some other useful **accents** are: Alt+129=ü, +130=é, +131=â, +133=à, +134=å, +135=ç +136=ê, +138=è, +139=ï, +145=æ, +147=ô and +184=©.

EXERCISE 16

PAINT

The program Paint is found by going ⊞ start – **All Programs – Accessories – Paint**. An art gallery would be needed to illustrate all that the Paint program can do.

When you open Paint, the **Tool Box** is probably showing. If it isn't, a ✓ is required in the **View** Menu. The same goes for the **Color Box**. If you put the tip of your mouse arrow exactly at the very edge of the tool box or the color box, you can drag them about. The pencil Button ✏ is already, that is to say, by default, pressed in for action. You draw by dragging the mouse.

Rest your mouse arrow on each of the Buttons along the tool box in turn, allowing each one enough time to display its function. You can make the drawing easier to see on the screen by magnifying a section of it by putting the **magnifier** 🔍 over it. To reverse the magnification, click **View – Zoom – Normal Size**.

When you have produced something you like, save it before doing any more experimenting which might spoil it.

Until there is something selected on your drawing board, **Cut** and **Copy** on the **Edit** Menu will be dimmed out. Selecting something in Paint is what is often called highlighting in Files containing text. To select a drawing, click the **Select** Button on the tool box. Dragging the mouse pointer ✛, now cross-shaped, from top left of the drawing to bottom right will draw a rectangle to enclose it. What is in the rectangle is now selected. To select only part of a drawing, click **Free-Form Select**. Once an area is selected, you can copy and paste it elsewhere or drag it about the drawing board. To delete what you've selected, put the pointer in the dotted rectangle and press **Delete**. To get rid of such selections, click anywhere.

The **A** Button, when pointed at, declares itself to be **Text**. If you click it, your mouse pointer ✛, when dragged from upper left to lower right will make an oblong in which typed letters will be accepted. You need the text Toolbar for this. If it's not showing, click the **View** Menu and give **Text Toolbar** a tick. You will be offered a choice of font, point size, underline, italic and bold. There are two squares to the left of the color box. To print in a colour, left-click the colour on the Color Box and the front square will show that colour. If you right-click a colour, the back square, usually white, will change to that colour. The background of the text rectangle will now change to that colour. To get rid of a text rectangle, but leave what you've typed, click anywhere.

If you want to use the **Undo** command but the **Edit** Menu which contains it is hidden by the text Toolbar, instead of clicking away the text Toolbar, it is easier to revert to the pre-mouse era and type **Ctrl+Z** which is the keyboard shortcut for **Undo**.

If you want to set the size of the picture when printed, choose **Attributes** in the **Image** Menu and fill in the required dimensions. You can alter the size of a drawing by selecting it and using the **Image** Menu.

To colour a space enclosed within a line, for example a circle drawn with the **Ellipse** tool, click on a colour and on the **Fill with color** Button. Move over the space and click there. If more space than you expect gets coloured, there's probably a gap in the line around the space, allowing the paint to leak out. If you can't see a gap, click on the magnifier and click again to find the leak.

Trouble-Shooting in Paint

If your screen remains blank with only the mouse arrow ✛ showing on it, do basic first aid. Click the left clicker and, if that doesn't work, the right.

If nothing appears when you draw, perhaps what you are drawing is in the same colour as the background. You can do this deliberately, for instance, by clicking white as a colour and using the **Brush** to erase other colours on a white background.

EXERCISE 17

PRINTING

Ask whoever installs your PC to install a printer at the same time. It can be a daunting procedure because you have to plug it in to the back of your machine and may have to follow "jargonese" instructions.

Print Preview (Not always available)
This item on the **File** Menu of a **WordPad** document (or a Button ⧉ on the Toolbar) will show what the printed page will look like.

Page Setup
This item on the **File** Menu of a **WordPad** document will offer a choice of paper size, a choice of margin width, and whether you want portrait ☐ or landscape ☐ orientation. (On other word-processing systems, look in the **File** Menu for items like **Document properties**.)

Wysiwyg

This means, "What You See Is What You Get". What your printer prints may vary in size from what's on your screen. A change of point size can counteract this so as to achieve "wysiwyg".

To Start Printing

If you choose the print Button *from the Toolbar*, printing may start at once. If, however, you choose **Print** *from the* **File** *Menu*, the Print window gives you a choice for selecting the particular pages of a document that you want printed, the number of copies and the quality of print. Different printers will offer different options for printing, so it is best to refer to the handbook which accompanied your printer.

EXERCISE 18

CDs, CD-ROMs AND DVDs

Playing a Music CD

To play a CD (**Compact Disc**) you need a CD slot to put it in (usually known as **Drive [D:]**) and loudspeakers. Press the Button just below the CD-ROM slot and a tray will come out or a door will open. (Other controls there refer to an extension loudspeaker.) Put a CD on the tray, labelled side up, and press the Button to make the tray go back into the machine, carrying the disk with it. The CD driver may be sluggish and you may have to wait several seconds until the little light below the slot stops flickering and the music starts.

The **Audio CD (D:)** window will appear, the computer having recognized that you have inserted a music CD. It will ask you what you want to do. Click on **Play audio CD using Windows Media Player** and click **OK**. Your music CD will then play. You can pause the music by clicking on the left handmost button near the bottom left of the screen, then continue the music by clicking that pause/play button

again. To stop the music completely, click the small square
button beside the pause/play button.

Sounds and Audio Devices Properties

| Volume | Sounds | Audio | Voice | Hardware |

Realtek HD Audio output

Device volume

Low   High

☐ Mute

☑ Place volume icon in the taskbar

Advanced...

Speaker settings

Use the settings below to change individual
speaker volume and other settings.

Speaker Volume...   Advanced...

OK   Cancel   Apply

If you can't hear anything, check that **Mute** isn't ticked.
To see **Mute**, double-click the **Sounds and Audio
Devices** icon in your Control Panel. If **Mute** is ticked,
untick it with a click. (Ticking **Mute** comes in useful to
silence a CD when the phone rings or to stop aural inanities
coming from a CD-ROM.) You can drag the slider to adjust
volume.

If you ❌ the CD Player window or close it by other means, the program shuts down, but, if you just minimize it down to the taskbar, the music keeps going.

Playing a CD-ROM

Whereas music CDs play sounds only, CD-ROMs may also include text and illustrations. Some CD-ROMs come with instructions printed on the packaging. Most supply on-screen instructions when you start playing them. These step-by-step instructions are known as a wizard, so all you have to do is to glance at the screen to see what it says and press **Next**.

When a piece of software from a CD-ROM, such as that in Windows or word-processing programs, is needed at all times, the **software** from these CD-ROMs should be **installed**, that is to say, incorporated into your machine by being transferred on to its **hard drive.**

To install anything, put the CD in and follow the instructions that appear on the screen. (If nothing happens, go to **My Computer** and double-click on (**D:**). To remove or uninstall something from the hard drive, follow the uninstallation program, if there is one. Otherwise go **start** – **Control Panel** – **Add/Remove programs**. Scroll to find the program and click **Remove**.

Even if you install, only temporarily, CD-ROM software, such as a game, and then uninstall it, doing this sometimes still leaves your machine cluttered up with a residue of unwanted Files. They don't do any harm, so only delete them if you know what you're doing.

If there is **no response** from a CD-ROM, press on the

Button below the CD slot, wait for the tray to come out and then press the Button again. That will restart it.

Playing a DVD

If your computer has the correct software, you can watch films recorded onto DVDs. Insert the DVD in the same way as you would a CD. The **DVD (D:)** window automatically appears, asking you what you want to do. Click on **Play DVD Video using Windows Media Player** and click **OK**. Windows Media Player will open and start playing the film.

Copying files onto a CD or DVD

Insert a writable or rewritable CD into the computer. After a few moments the **CD Drive (D:)** window appears asking you what you want to do.

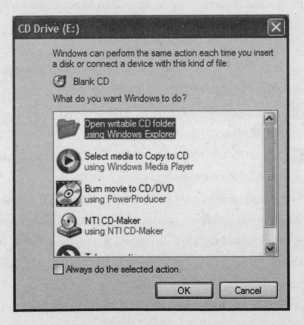

The computer will recognize that you have inserted a blank CD and highlight the option **Open writable CD folder using Windows Explorer**. Click on **OK**, and the **CD Writing Tasks** Menu will open, offering you some options including the one **Write these Files to CD.**

Minimize this window, then open Windows Explorer (by right-clicking **Start** and choosing **Explore**). Find the File or Folder you wish to copy to the CD, right-click it and choose **Copy** from the menu.

Maximize the **CD Drive (D:)** window, right-click in the white empty space and choose **Paste**. Your chosen File or Folder will now appear faintly under **Files Ready to Be Written to the CD.**

In the left-hand column click on **Write these Files to CD**. The **CD Writing Wizard** now appears. In the highlighted box, type the name you want to give to the CD. Then click **Next** at the bottom of the box. The File/Folder will now be written to the CD. This will take a few minutes. When it has finished saving the File/Folder, the CD tray will automatically open so that you can remove the CD.

Follow the same procedure if your computer is capable of saving data to a DVD.

Changing the Screen Resolution

Sometimes a piece of software which you install prefers a larger screen than you can offer it, making necessary a change in **screen resolution**. In that case you need the program called Display, which is on the Control Panel window (**start** – **Control Panel**). Click the **Settings** tab on the Display window and drag the **Desktop area** slider from **Less to More**, from a lower number of **pixels** (little dots which occupy the whole of your screen like the dots on a newspaper picture), to a larger number on the right. That means that more pixels, smaller ones, can be crammed onto the same-sized screen. Then click any **OK** or **Yes** which appears. Reverse the process when you want to revert to normal, starting from the **Settings** tab on the Display window.

Looking After Your Disks

Keep CDs and DVDs protected when not in use by keeping them in their boxes or in plastic envelopes. Grease from fingers can confuse the laser beam which scans them.

EXERCISE 19

WHAT IS THE INTERNET?

The world-wide network of telephones is such that you can telephone anybody with a telephone anywhere on Planet Earth. A computer connected to a telephone can also communicate with any other computer connected to a telephone, anywhere on Planet Earth. That world-wide network of computers, connected to each other by telephone wire, is the basis of the Internet.

The Internet is not just an empty network, because people use it as a display board on which to stick things. Anybody joined up to the Internet can see what's been stuck there. This part of the Internet is called the World Wide Web, the www. What is on display, like the postcards in the window of the local shop, reflects human supply and demand.

The www is a library, an art gallery, a music library, a notice board, a porn shop, a shopping mall, a debating society, a newspaper, a lonely hearts club, a mail-order catalogue, a conference of professors, a sporting stadium, a gaming gallery, a railway time-table, a theatre box office, an estate agent – you name it. It is made up of what people have put onto it.

To do this they have each set up a **web site** and given it an address so that other people can find it. If you did this to advertise your old sofa-bed, everybody joined to the Internet becomes a potential customer. Setting up a web site requires specialist skills which are beyond the scope of this book.

You can't telephone anybody direct without going through a telephone exchange, even if it's an automatic one. Your computer, likewise, needs an intermediary. It is called an ISP, an **Internet Service Provider**. So if you want to get connected to the Internet, your first need is an ISP connected to you by telephone. For most home users there are two main levels of service: "dial-up" and **broadband**. Broadband is much faster and cleverly shares the telephone line so that you can make calls at the same time as using the Internet, which dial-up does not. The cost of broadband continues to fall and, for most people, it is the preferable option, although you will need to check with the ISP that it's available in your area.

The modem

The gadget in (or plugged into) your computer which connects you by telephone to your ISP is called a **modem**. It works by translating the digital electrical signals of your computer into signals which can be sent along a telephone line. When they reach their destination they are translated back to the digital electrical signals understood by computers.

Internet Service Providers

There are dozens of them. Most now offer broadband, as well as dial-up. There is no way you can be sure that the ISP you chose is the best one for you because they are all different. Some charge you by the hour, some by the month, some have different rates according to the time of day, some are free and earn their keep by advertising, some are fast, some are slow, some suit occasional users, some suit persistent users and so on. No matter; you can easily change later on to another one. Take advantage of the facilities offered by your ISP, such as parental control to protect your children from the pornography which flourishes world wide.

If you aren't provided with an ISP's software in your PC package, ask a friend to recommend one. Read carefully any literature that comes with the installation CD-Rom and note its helpline telephone number in case you get stuck. To start again, perform **Uninstall** (see Index).

Installing an ISP's Software

Right-click on any Buttons on your taskbar and click **Close** to clear them all away, and, when you have some time to spare, put into the slot the CD-ROM provided by the ISP. (A CD-ROM often starts automatically when it goes into the machine. If it's in the machine, but not working, press the Button below the slot, wait for the tray to come out and then press the Button again to send it back in.) You are going to install this software onto your hard disk. Follow very carefully the instruction on your screen (the **"wizard"**). Make a note of your username and password in case you get stuck and have to start again.

"Signing up" is what you do when you register with an ISP. (Signing on is connecting to the Internet, also known as being on-line, being connected or logged on.) If you get stuck, start again and have another go. If the installation is complete but it still doesn't work, uninstall it and start again, if necessary telephoning the helpline.

Once an ISP's software has been installed, its icon will probably appear on your Desktop or on your taskbar. Double-click it and you will be shown a browser. Here is one, **Internet Explorer,** the one that comes ready-installed with Windows.

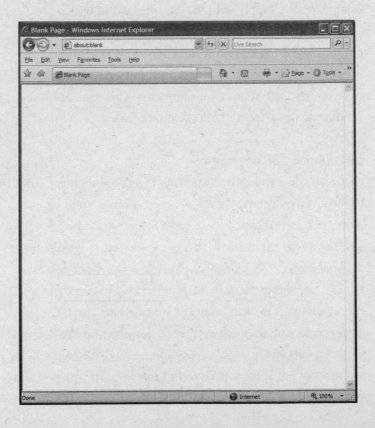

There are others, such as Netscape. A **browser** is a program which allows you to view the Internet. It has a row of icons – a dashboard of switches for choosing what you want to do with the Internet. Some of them will be dimmed out unless you are on-line.

Going On-line
Clicking the ISP icon or the browser icon on your Desktop should bring up a box like this:

If the **Save Password** box in that Dial-up Connection window is ticked, you won't have to type in your password every time you go on-line. If **Connect automatically** is ticked (not always present), you will go on-line when you click your ISP icon on the Desktop, or when you press **Enter** after typing a web site address. If you're not on-line and wish to be so, you may have to look for **Connect** or **Go On-line** and click there (though with broadband you remain connected right up until you switch your PC off).

To see what's on a web site, type its address, if you know it, in the **Address** or **Location** box on your browser. A web site may consist of a **page** or many pages. Its address starts with **http://www** although you can just type www and the rest will be added automatically by the browser. The address must be typed exactly; a space, or a comma instead of a full stop, will spoil it.

Press the **Enter** key, and the information at that address gets **downloaded** onto your screen. What appears is the first page at that address. Clicking something underlined or highlighted on a web page – a **link** – will open another page.

The controls on your browser are for manipulating what's now on your screen. Here are some of the controls on Internet Explorer:

Once you have clicked through a few pages on a web site, you may wish to return to those previously visited. To do this, click the **Back** button ⬅ . Once you have clicked **Back**, you may click **Forward** ➡ to return to those pages already visited.

Click **Stop** ⊠ if the pages of a web site are aggravatingly slow in appearing (in being downloaded). You can stop the process with the **Stop** Button and either click **Refresh** ⟳ , or go to a different web site. (You could ask your dealer to install a faster modem to speed things up.)

A **Search icon** 🔍▾ on a browser will allow you to

search the web for web sites containing a **keyword** which you have typed in. It may not find what you want, but may be a simple route to start looking for something.

Favorites ☆ lets you record a web site address which you can find quickly next time you go on-line. To do this, have it downloaded, i.e. showing on your screen, click **Favorites**, then click **Add to Favorites** and then **Add**. When you next go on-line and click **Favorites**, the one you have added to your list will be shown there for you to click open.

Clicking **Print** 🖶 prints what you see on screen.

Search Engines

There are dozens of these, accessible by typing in their www addresses. They scour the web for topics. What they find depends on what they have been furnished with, so results vary.

Try typing, in the address box on the browser, the address **www.google.co.uk**, a search engine. A page will appear containing a query box where you can type a word or subject which you wish to find information about on the Internet. Pressing **Enter** will open a page containing the results of your search – a list of web sites which contain the word or words that you entered in the query box. Click on one of these and you will be taken to that web site. Try typing **Constable & Robinson** in the query box. As well as pressing **Enter**, you can click **Google Search** or **I'm Feeling Lucky**. Try searching using both of these. Go down to the bottom of the Google page and click **About Google**. Click **Help and How to Search** and there appears a page

of tips on improving your method of searching which could
save yourself a lot of trouble.

Storing What You've Downloaded
When a web site is showing on your screen, click **Save As**
on the File Menu, and treat what's on your screen as you
would a File you wanted to save.

Groups, Chatrooms and Blogs
These are discussion groups, interested in any subject from
pigeon racing to philosophy. They communicate mostly by
e-mail. There are thousands of them. Try clicking Groups
on **www.google.co.uk**

There are also Chat Rooms (sometimes called channels),
web sites where people can type in conversations. There
used to be pen-pals; now there are Internet pals. A weblog,
usually shortened to blog, is a web site where regular entries
are made, like a diary. Often including images and links to
other blogs, many allow readers to leave comments or
opinions on the blog's subject. To learn more about all these
things, look at a web site like **www.yahoo.com**, or use a
search engine like Google.

EXERCISE 20

E-MAIL

E-mail is a method of sending text, images or programs along telephone lines, via the Internet. To engage in e-mail you must use an e-mail program, or mail client. The one supplied with Internet Explorer is called **Outlook Express**. The Netscape browser comes with a mail client called Netscape messenger.

To open your e-mail program either double-click its icon in the **Start** Menu or, if there is one, double-click its

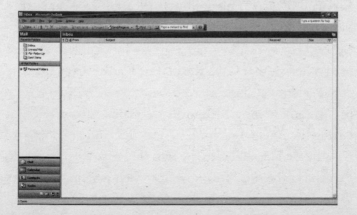

shortcut on your Desktop (see page 81 to remind you how to make a shortcut).

Sending E-mail

Look for the icon **Create Mail**, **New Msg** or **New Mail**. Clicking one of these gives you a blank area for you to type in your message. These icons are clickable before you connect to the Internet, so that you can compose your message at leisure without paying for the time taken. You can also type your message in your word-processing program and, using **Select** and **Copy**, paste it into your e-mail window.

Practise the art of sending e-mails by addressing one to yourself. You will be given an e-mail address by your ISP when you sign up with one. In the **To** box of the e-mail window, type in the **e-mail address** of the person you're sending it to. An e-mail address looks like joeblogs@provider.com. It begins with a name – note that there are no spaces anywhere in joeblogs – followed by an @ (pronounced "at") followed by the name of an Internet Service Provider. This followed by a full stop and other letters such as **com** or **co.uk**. Type in something in the **Subject** box so that in future you can distinguish this e-mail from others. Either leave the **cc** box blank or type in it the e-mail address of someone you want to send a carbon copy to. To send a **copy to another e-mail address**, without letting the original recipient know that you are doing so, type the second address in the **bcc** (blind carbon copy) box. Remember the slick **Tab key** ⇄ when jumping from box to box.

Now that you've composed your message off-line, click **Send/Receive** 🖳Send/Receive and it will be put into your **Outbox**. Click 🖳Send/Receive and then click **Connect** in the **Dial-up Connection** box which then appears. When your e-mail has been sent, a copy will remain in your **Sent** folder.

If you want to send a picture you have to attach it to your e-mail as a separate File called an **attachment**. To do this click **Attach** 📎 on your e-mail form. Find the File you wish to attach from the **Look in** window. Click **Attach** and send the e-mail in the usual way.

Receiving E-Mail

Your new e-mail messages are stored by your Internet Service Provider until you go on-line to check if there are any waiting for you. Once you have checked for new e-mail, it will be listed in your **Inbox** Folder. You can then go off-line and read it at your leisure.

To reply to an e-mail, highlight its name in the Inbox, then click on the **Reply** 🔁Reply icon. Type your reply and click **Send**.

If the original e-mail that you received was sent to more than one person, you can click on **Reply All** 🔁Reply to All so that everyone who got the original message can receive your reply.

To pass an e-mail you've received on to another person, highlight the message and click on the **Forward** 🔁Forward icon, then type in the recipient's e-mail address in the **To** box and click **Send**.

In order to **view an attachment** to an e-mail, you need to download it, to get it into your machine from the outside world. First you must have on screen the e-mail to which it is attached. Click the paperclip icon in the right-hand corner and you'll see a list of attachments which open if you click on them. Clicking **Save Attachments** at the bottom of the list, puts you in the same position as you were when, with the **Save As** window open, you chose a storage site for a new document. Note the name of the attached File and the Folder where you choose to store it (click Browse and pick somewhere to store it, which then shows in the **Save To** box). Click **Save**. Then you can find the document by clicking its icon on the Desktop, by **Find Files or Folders** on the **Start** Menu or by following the path to it, Folder by Folder as described on page 75. You can then open it and see it on screen. If the attached File is different in type from your usual ones, there might be problems in viewing it but these are beyond the scope of this guide. Trawl your ISP information material or use its helpline phone number.

When opening e-mail attachments, you must always be aware of the risks posed by computer viruses. Many viruses are sent by people who do not realize that they are sending them, and often they can do a lot of harm to your computer. One way to arm yourself against this threat is to invest in some anti-virus software which will detect any known viruses contained in an e-mail attachment (or on any disk which you put into the computer) and eradicate them. Something called a Firewall is a program and/or a bit of equipment which does much the same job.

Another way is always to be very cautious when receiving attachments, especially those with suspicious-sounding file names. If you receive an e-mail with an attachment which you think may contain a virus, delete the e-mail without opening the attachment and contact the person who sent it to you. If you receive an e-mail with an attachment from somebody you don't know, just delete it straight away without opening it or the attachment.

EXERCISE 21

UNSOLICITED GIFTS

You will only use a tiny fraction of what your PC offers, simply because a kindly feature of computer designers is their persistent wish to please everybody all the time in all circumstances. They insist, for instance, that you should be able to decide the vital issue of whether your Desktop should appear plain or stripy. (See **Start– Control Panel – Display – Desktop tab.**)

You must learn to stand on your own two feet and make your own selections. You may, for instance, see in you **Start** Menu, these icons:

 My Documents    My Pictures

They're just empty Folders into which you can sort Files or other Folders, in the usual way, by dragging or saving into them. You can make your own – right-click on the Desktop or on a window listing the names of Files or Folders, click | New   ▸ | and 🗀 Folder .

EXERCISE 22

EXTRAS AND SAFETY PRECAUTIONS

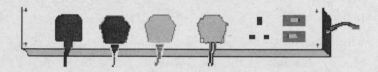

Ideally, there is interposed between your machine and mains electricity not just an **"anti-surge"** device but also an "anti-peak" device, to protect against harmful variations in your local power supply. These devices are often incorporated in the sort of multi-socket strip used for plugging in several items. This safeguard is perhaps more necessary in the country than in cities, but is good insurance. As a further hazard, when your computer is plugged in, electricity from a thunderstorm miles away can damage it even if it's switched off, so unplug from the mains in stormy weather.

Unplug also, during thunderstorms or before you go on holiday, your printer from the mains and your modem from its telephone line. My local computer shop has today six melted modems and a damaged printer. You will see a wire from the back of your computer plugged in to a telephone socket in the wall. That wire comes from your modem.

One bit of maintenance you can do yourself is to **defragment**. Removing stuff from the Recycle Bin leaves untidy gaps in your machine which slows it down. Defragmentation from time to time is the answer. To do this go Start – All Programs – Accessories – System Tools – Disk Defragmenter and follow the instructions. It may take quite a long time to run.

It might be useful for you to swap a 14 inch monitor for a larger one or to buy some more **RAM** (Random Access Memory), if your supplier says it will lessen the time that little hourglass ⌛ keeps you waiting. I had endless trouble with illegal operations and text going haywire when working on this book, until I discovered that my machine didn't have enough RAM to cope with the vast number of bytes needed for the numerous illustrations.

There's a whole world of extras for you to spend your money on. You might like a **scanner**, which can transfer pictures or text onto your screen for printing or modifying – removing red eye from a photograph for instance. With a **digital camera** red eye is largely a thing of the past. Connect it to your computer and your photographs can be viewed on-screen leaving you free to print copies of your best ones. Digital movie cameras, or camcorders, work in much the same way, recording and storing your home movies as computer files.

MP3 players are like the old "Walkman" personal stereos, with the music stored on them as computer files rather than on tapes or CDs. The best known player is, of course, the iPod. You might find a **Portable Storage Device** worth buying. These are, simply, scaled-down hard disks which you plug into your computer and copy, delete, save or move files to and from as you would with your computer's own hard disk. With many as small as a key fob, they're great for moving lots of files from one computer to another.

As you might imagine, there are amazing games and miraculous devices being invented as fast as anyone can think of them.

PART TWO

WINDOWS VISTA

INTRODUCTION

Ever since Microsoft launched its new operating system Windows Vista at the beginning of 2007, it has received what might charitably be called a mixed response. On the one hand, some people in the know say that it's too like Windows XP and isn't really a new system at all. But on the other hand, people have complained that there have been too many changes. It would seem hard to believe they can both be right.

For what it's worth, I tend to side with those who are in the latter camp. I suspect there have been too many unnecessary changes, that there are too many compatibility issues between Vista and various pieces of hardware (by which I actually mean they are incompatible) and that there is a severe shortage of proper drivers to get things working. However, this is all down to my personal opinion and does not alter the task – my business is to make things easy for you on your PC and, if you have Vista loaded, then there are plenty of ways to make it fully operational for your purposes. The majority of the skills you will have learned from using Windows XP are still relevant with Vista so I am going to assume that you do not need reminding of simple tasks such as single-clicking, closing windows, etc. By and large, the problems tend to crop up with advanced features, so they generally need not concern us. However, I will shortly take an example of Vista's functionality within this introduction and demonstrate in an exercise how to get everything running smoothly.

There are several different editions of Vista which, broadly speaking, we can divide into those aimed at home and business users. I shall be dealing with the principal versions for home use, namely Vista Home Basic and Vista Home Premium, whereas Vista Business and Vista Ultimate are obviously designed for the latter market. There is also a version called Vista Starter which is only for sale in emerging markets – that is to say, not in countries in the developed world so you are unlikely to be able to get hold of it.

One of the most common problems for all editions reported by critics since the 2007 launch (and which I initially suffered from myself) is not knowing how to add or remove certain features to or from Vista. You might well be in the same boat. To answer your questions and help you customize the Vista features the way you want to, I am going to show you how to do this in an introductory exercise. Even though the procedure has certain similarities to Windows XP, in Vista there is a key difference.

In Windows XP and earlier versions, in order to turn a feature off you had to uninstall it completely from your PC. In Vista, all the features remain stored on your hard disk, so you can turn them back on quickly if you want to. This can be an advantage since you don't have to look for and insert the Vista DVD every time you want to turn on a particular feature. However, there is another potentially harmful side of the coin because you won't be able to save any disk space by removing the features you don't need. It seems that, in this case, Microsoft definitely traded ease of use for the loss of hard disk space.

At first glance, the **Add/Remove Programs** section is nowhere to be found. Don't despair – it's just been renamed. Instead, if you want to turn Vista features on or off, you have to do it from the **Programs and Features** box. Fortunately, this is relatively simple to locate. First, go to **Control Panel**. At the foot of the page on the left-hand side you will see a section called **Programs** and beneath it you will find two choices: the first is the **Uninstall a program** option. Click on it and you will be turning off the program (uninstalling

it is in fact a misnomer). The alternative choice you have is to **Change startup programs** i.e. add a program.

Another of the ways to find this facility is to search for the word **programs** in the Start Menu search box.

In the **Programs and Features** window, click on **Turn Windows features on or off**. Let me add a quick word of warning at this point: if something called UAC (User Account Control) is enabled you might need to make an additional confirmation. This is one of those Vista features that have proved controversial because it often slows things down (and sometimes even prevents desired changes occurring). Be sure you've got your password handy because you might need it to confirm the action.

Now you will see a list with all the available Vista features. Some features are grouped together in folders, and some folders contain subfolders with additional features. If you want to view the contents of a folder, you must double-click it or click on the + sign.

If a check box of a folder is partially checked or appears dark, then some of the items inside it are enabled and some are disabled. If a feature is fully checked then it has been already enabled. The features that are not checked are disabled.

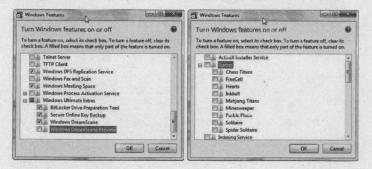

Let's say that you want to disable one of the features in the folder marked Windows Ultimate Extras. As you can see from the screenshot on the left, both the Windows DreamScene Preview and the final version are listed as having been installed. You can now disable the Preview version (as it's no longer needed) by clearing its box.

In addition, let's assume that you would like to disable all the pre-loaded Vista Games (having played most of them on XP if you recall earlier exercises). So just scroll up to the Games folder (above right) and deselect it.

In this way, you can enable or disable any of the listed Vista features. After you have decided what you'd like to add or remove from your PC, click on *OK*. Vista will then perform the appropriate actions – but remember the features will still be stored on disk.

Wait until the progress bar disappears. Then, the screen will probably ask you to restart your PC so that the changes you've set up can be implemented in the system.

Not so bad, is it? The only problem is that available disk space is always contracting, never expanding, so make sure you really need a program before adding it.

Mike Hobbs

EXERCISE 23

MANIPULATING WINDOWS

As I've already shown in the introduction, one of the most visible changes that you'll find in Vista is the complete redesign of the Control Panel. Basically, lots of things have been moved and although now you have very easy access to some configuration options it is equally true to say that others seem to have been hidden deep in the new Control Panel menus.

If, like me, you have a hard time finding things and yearn for the classic way of working developed for the earlier operating systems, don't worry. Vista gives you the option to switch back to the old Control Panel and this is how you do it: go to **Start** 🌀 – **Control Panel**.

If you look carefully at the layout I showed you in the introduction (page 127), you will notice that on the top left-hand side of the screen there is a panel with two options. The first option is **Control Panel Home** and the second is **Classic View**.

Click on **Classic View** and the Control Panel will be

reloaded and will look just like the old one from Windows
2000 and XP (below right).

So now everything has been put back into alphabetical
order. Personally, I'm happier with this layout because I'm
used to it, but of course the choice is up to you.

Another of the biggest changes in Vista that you'll notice
almost instantly is the complete redesign of the Start Menu.
Again, some people may not mind this, but I'm a creature of
habit and prefer to use the old style Start Menu. In this
exercise I will show you how to enable and configure the
classic version of the Start Menu, as used in Windows XP.
This makes it consistent with the Classic View Control
Panel.

First, right-click on your taskbar (in the bottom left-hand
corner of the screen) and select **Properties**.

The Taskbar and Start Menu Properties window will open. Go to the **Start Menu** tab and check the **Classic Start Menu** option. If you want to customize the items that appear in the Start Menu, click the **Customize...** button. This is useful for advanced PC users but adds further complications that might be unnecessary for the moment, so let's assume you don't want to customize anything – in that case, you would just press the **OK** button.

But if you do want to play around (and why not?), you can have your wish. In the **Customize Classic Start Menu** window you'll find you have lots of configuration options: you can add or remove start menu items, you can sort them or you can enable special shortcuts like the **Run** or **Log Off** buttons.

Feel free to experiment with all the available options. If you don't want to implement any of the proposed customized changes, leave the options as they stand. When you have finished, press the *OK* button.

Now your Vista Start Menu will look just like the older versions of Windows, and as a result, make it easier if you wish to follow the exercises that have been set out earlier in the book.

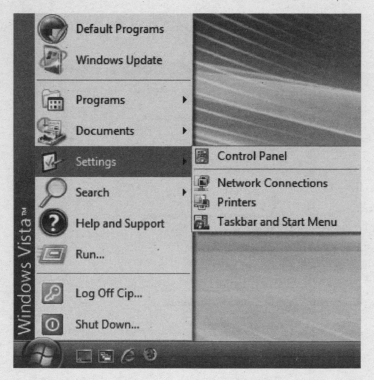

EXERCISE 24

SHUTTING DOWN

Another potentially confusing change in Vista is the redesign of the way in which you can shut down your PC. The **Log Off** and **Shut Down** buttons are no longer in the same position and even if the new **Sleep** and **Lock Computer** buttons in Vista give you the impression that they have the same functionality, they don't.

However, if you take a closer look at the **Start Menu** 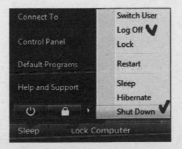, you will see that to the right of those two big buttons there is a small "arrow like" button. If you press on it, a menu with seven options will appear. **Log Off** is the second from the top and **Shut Down** is the last.

There you have it – confusing but not impossible. Yet should you switch off your machine? The experts still don't agree. Some people never turn their computers off, swearing that keeping the temperature constant is crucial, and that the wear and tear from switching on and off is damaging. Others say it is destructive to leave it on all the time because the monitor decays and the computer's components overheat. Personally, I still turn mine off at night and when leaving the house.

EXERCISE 25

CHOOSING PROGRAMS

In this short exercise I am going to show you how to set the default programs that Vista will use to open certain files or protocols (a protocol in computerspeak, as in real life, is basically a set way of doing things, in this case presenting information). This will be very useful to you especially when you install similar programs on your PC and you want to open certain things with an application and others with a secondary application.

In the **Start Menu** – **Search** box type the word **default** and then click on the first result.

The **Default Programs** main window will open and you will see four options. Please note that is the new Screen Layout and not the Classic Look that I showed you how to set up on page 131.

Choose the programs that Windows uses by default

Set your default programs
Make a program the default for all file types and protocols it can open.

You'll see you have four options. Click on the top line for the **Set your default programs** link. This is going to save you a lot of time and trouble later. After a short **Loading...** screen you will see a list with all the programs that you can configure.

Here you can set a program as default for a specific file type, extension or protocol. Let's pick **Internet Explorer** as an example. Click on it and on the right side of the window you will see a small description of the program and what it can do for you. Lower down the page, there will be a note that informs you of Internet Explorer's current status on your PC. In other words it tells you how many of all the file types and protocols it could possibly open are actually set for it to open by default at the moment.

 Internet Explorer
Microsoft Windows

Windows Internet Explorer 7 provides an easier and more secure web browsing experience. Perform quick searches right from the toolbar, custom print your webpages, and discover, manage, and read RSS feeds.

This program has 3 out of 9 defaults

So, as you can see in this example, Internet Explorer is set as the default opener for three out of a total of nine possibilities. If you want to set this program as default for every file type, protocol or extension it can open, click on the Set this program as default link.

Set this program as default
Use the selected program to open all file types and protocols it can open by default.

When you have finished, click on OK. It will now open every possible type. If you want to be more selective and edit the number of file types a program will open by default, select it and then click the Choose defaults for this program link.

Choose defaults for this program
Choose which file types and protocols the selected program opens by default.

A new window will open where you can see all the possibilities and set the program associations.

Here you can see all file types, extensions and protocols that Internet Explorer can open for you by default. If you want Internet Explorer to be the default for a specific extension or protocol, check the appropriate box right next to it. After you have made your selections click on **Save** and then on **OK**. If you want to carry out further exercises relating to choosing programs, please go back to page 33.

EXERCISE 26

MOVING AND COPYING
FILES OR FOLDERS

One of the best tips I can pass on to you is never to keep your personal files and folders (such as My Documents, My Music, My Pictures, etc) in their default locations. In Vista, all the personal folders are stored on the drive where the operating system is installed. By leaving them in their default location, each time you have problems with the operating system there is a risk that you might lose them. If something happens and you need to format the C drive that means all your documents, music and pictures will be lost.

To avoid such problems you can always move them and store everything on a separate partition. This way, you can format the C drive and reinstall the operating system as many times as you need without risking your data. Generally, it is always better to keep only the operating system and the applications you use on your C drive. All of your data, including documents or saved games should be kept elsewhere.

In this exercise I will show you how to move your personal files and folders to other partitions.

The user folders that can be moved are the following: **Contacts, Documents, Downloads, Favorites, Links, Music, Pictures, Saved Games, Searches** and **Videos**. To find them go to your user folder. You will find it on the partition where you installed Vista, in the ***Users*** folder. Its name will be the same as your user. You can move as many folders as you need. Just select them one by one and follow the instructions.

First of all, right-click on the folder you want to move and select **Properties**.

Documen   **Explore**   ds

Open

Search...

7-Zip   ▶

Share...

Restore previous versions

Scan with AVG

Videos   Send To   ▶   OG

Cut

Copy

Create Shortcut

Delete

Rename

Properties

Now go to the **Location** tab. Here you will see the current location of your selected folder. To change it, click on **Move**.

Next, you should browse your PC and select the preferred new location.

When you've accomplished this to your satisfaction, click on **Apply**.

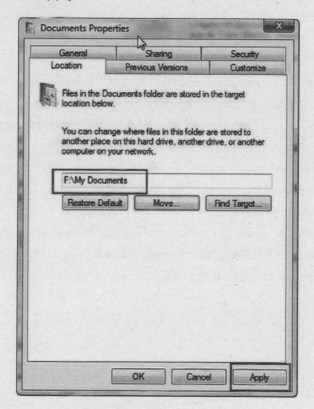

Now you will be asked if you want to move all the files from the current location to the new one. (In cases where you have second thoughts, you can click on **No**.)

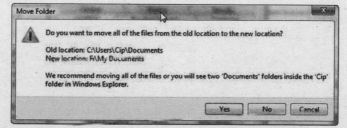

Otherwise click on **Yes** and wait until all the files have been transferred to the new location. Depending on how many files you selected, the moving procedure can take from a few seconds up to quite a few minutes.

My personal advice is that you move your user folders shortly after you have installed Vista. If you do it after you have installed many applications and your PC has been used a lot, you might have problems because some references will remain in the old locations of your user folders. These references might cause some applications not to work properly and you might therefore need to reinstall them – a hassle you can avoid.

If you wish to go over some elementary details concerning moving and copying files, please go back to the exercises starting on page 71.

EXERCISE 27

FINDING, DELETING AND RESTORING FILES

One of the first things I do after I install any Windows Operating System is to make sure I have access to all hidden folders and that I can see the extension for all files, including common files like .txt or .doc. That is because I want to have complete access to every file or folder within my system.

To make these settings in Windows XP was pretty easy – while I was browsing through the folders on my system, I selected **Tools** and then **Folder Options** from the top menu of **Windows Explorer**. When I used Vista for the first time I was a bit surprised to see that the *Tools* menu is nowhere to be found in **Windows Explorer.** You may be having the same problem. So where did it disappear to?

It seems it has been hidden from the Windows Explorer default interface. In order to access it, press the **ALT** key on your keyboard and the old menu will appear.

Another fast way to find the **Folder Options** is to use

the search box from the start menu. Simply type **folder
options** in the search field and the first result should be the
Folder Options shortcut.

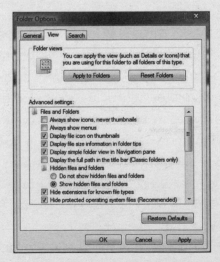

Next, click on the appropriate button or press the **Enter**
key to open it. Go to the **View** tab and make the settings
you want.

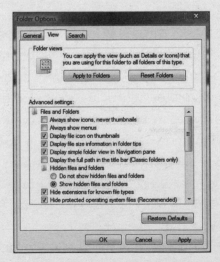

If you're using the new Control Panel, you need to go to **Appearance and Personalization** and then click on **Folder Options**. If, like me, you're using the Classic View you will see it in the list of items starting with the letter **f**.

Make your adjustments according to your wishes. Meanwhile, if you want more information about finding, deleting and restoring files and folders, please refer to the exercises beginning on page 75.

EXERCISE 28

Shortcuts

There are all sorts of shortcuts that you can take to enable you to work more quickly. I have discussed some of them in the chapters on Windows XP and covered them in exercises beginning on page 81. In addition there are also hundreds of shortcuts you can take on your keyboard that work in Vista as well as on earlier versions of Windows.

So here, without further ado, are some **General keyboard shortcuts:**

- **F1** – Display Help
- **CTRL+C** – Copy selected item
- **CTRL+X** – Cut selected item
- **CTRL+V** – Paste selected item
- **CTRL+Z** – Undo an action
- **CTRL+Y** – Redo an action
- **DELETE** – Delete selected item and move it to the Recycle Bin
- **SHIFT+DELETE** – Delete selected item without moving it to the Recycle Bin

- **F2** – Rename selected item
- **CTRL+RIGHT ARROW** – Move cursor to beginning of next word
- **CTRL+LEFT ARROW** – Move cursor to beginning of previous word
- **CTRL+DOWN ARROW** – Move cursor to beginning of next paragraph
- **CTRL+UP ARROW** – Move cursor to beginning of previous paragraph
- **CTRL+SHIFT with an arrow key** – Select a block of text
- **SHIFT with any arrow key** – Select more than one item in a window or on the desktop, or select text within a document
- **CTRL with any arrow key+SPACEBAR** – Select multiple individual items in a window or on the desktop
- **CTRL+A** – Select all items in a document or window
- **F3** – Search for a file or folder
- **ALT+ENTER** – Display properties for selected item
- **ALT+F4** – Close active item, or exit active program
- **ALT+SPACEBAR** – Open shortcut menu for active window
- **CTRL+F4** – Close active document (in programs that allow you to have multiple documents open simultaneously)
- **ALT+TAB** – Switch between open items
- **CTRL+ALT+TAB** – Use arrow keys to switch between open items
- **CTRL+Mouse scroll wheel** – Change size of icons on the desktop

- **Windows logo key + TAB** – Cycle through programs on the taskbar by using Windows Flip 3-D
- **CTRL+Windows logo key + TAB** – Use arrow keys to cycle through programs on the taskbar by using Windows Flip 3-D
- **ALT+ESC** – Cycle through items in the order in which they were opened
- **F6** – Cycle through screen elements in a window or on the desktop
- **F4** – Display Address Bar list in Windows Explorer
- **SHIFT+F10** – Display shortcut menu for the selected item
- **CTRL+ESC** – Open the Start menu
- **F10** – Activate menu bar in the active program
- **RIGHT ARROW** – Open next menu to the right, or open a submenu
- **LEFT ARROW** – Open next menu to the left, or close a submenu
- **F5** – Refresh the active window
- **ALT+UP ARROW** – View folder one level up in Windows Explorer
- **ESC** – Cancel the current task
- **CTRL+SHIFT+ESC** – Open Task Manager
- **SHIFT when you insert a CD** – Prevent the CD from automatically playing

These are some of the **Dialog box keyboard shortcuts:**
- **CTRL+TAB** – Move forward through tabs
- **CTRL+SHIFT+TAB** – Move back through tabs

- **TAB** – Move forward through options
- **SHIFT+TAB** – Move back through options
- **ALT+underlined letter** – Perform the command (or select the option) that goes with that letter
- **ENTER** – Replaces clicking the mouse for many selected commands
- **SPACEBAR** – Select or clear check box if the active option is a check box
- **Arrow keys** – Select button if the active option is a group of option buttons
- **F1** – Display Help
- **F4** – Display the items in the active list
- **BACKSPACE** – Open folder one level up if folder is selected in the Save As or Open dialog box

For advanced users, here are some **Windows Sidebar keyboard shortcuts:**

- **Windows logo key Picture of Windows logo key + SPACEBAR** – Bring all gadgets to the front and select Sidebar
- **Windows logo key Picture of Windows logo key +G** – Cycle through Sidebar gadgets
- **TAB** – Cycle through Sidebar controls

You can also check out these **Windows Explorer keyboard shortcuts:**

- **CTRL+N** – Open a new window
- **END** – Display the bottom of active window
- **HOME** – Display the top of active window
- **F11** – Maximize or minimize active window

- **LEFT ARROW** – Collapse the current selection (if it is expanded), or select parent folder
- **ALT+LEFT ARROW** – View previous folder
- **RIGHT ARROW** – Display the current selection (if it is collapsed), or select first subfolder
- **ALT+RIGHT ARROW** – View next folder
- **CTRL+Mouse scroll wheel** – Change size and appearance of file and folder icons
- **ALT+D** – Select the Address bar

You might need these **Windows Help viewer keyboard shortcuts:**

- **ALT+C** – Display Table of Contents
- **ALT+N** – Display Connection Settings menu
- **F10** – Display Options menu
- **ALT+LEFT ARROW** – Move back to previously viewed topic
- **ALT+RIGHT ARROW** – Move forward to next (previously viewed) topic
- **ALT+A** – Display the customer support page
- **ALT+HOME** – Display the Help and Support home page
- **HOME** – Move to beginning of a topic
- **END** – Move to end of a topic
- **CTRL+F** – Search current topic
- **CTRL+P** – Print a topic
- **F3** – Move to the Search box

Here are some more **General shortcuts:**
- Turn Full Screen Mode On or Off – **F11**

- Cycle through the Address Bar, Refresh button, Search Box, and items on a web page – TAB
- Find a word or phrase on a page – CTRL+F
- Open the current webpage in a new window – CTRL+N
- Print the page – CTRL+P
- Select all items on the page – CTRL+A
- Zoom in – CTRL+PLUS
- Zoom out – CTRL+MINUS
- Zoom to 100% – CTRL+0

Make your way with these **Navigation shortcuts:**
- Go to home page – ALT+HOME
- Go backward – ALT+LEFT
- Go forward – ALT+RIGHT
- Refresh page – F5
- Refresh page and the cache – CTRL+F5
- Stop downloading page – ESC

Save time with the following (American spelling) **Favorites Center shortcuts:**
- Open Favorites – CTRL+I
- Open Favorites in pinned mode – CTRL+SHIFT+I
- Organize Favorites – CTRL+B
- Add current page to Favorites – CTRL+D
- Open Feeds – CTRL+J
- Open Feeds in pinned mode – CTRL+SHIFT+J
- Open History – CTRL+H
- Open History in pinned mode – CTRL+SHIFT+H

Follow these **Tab shortcuts:**
- Open link in new background tab – CTRL+left mouse button
- Open link in new foreground tab – CTRL+SHIFT+left mouse button
- Close tab (closes window if only one tab is open) – CTRL+W
- Open Quick Tab view – CTRL+Q
- Open new tab – CTRL+T
- Switch to next tab – CTRL+TAB
- Switch to previous tab – CTRL+SHIFT+TAB

You can use these **Address Bar shortcuts:**
- Select the Address Bar – ALT+D
- Open website address typed in the Address Bar in new tab – ALT+ENTER
- View list of previously typed addresses – F4

Find shortcuts to the **Instant Search Box:**
- Select the Instant Search Box – CTRL+E
- View list of search providers – CTRL+DOWN
- Open search results in new tab – ALT+ENTER

Check out these **Shortcuts for use in main window:**
- Send and receive e mail – CTRL+M
- Open or post a new message – CTRL+N
- Open Contacts – CTRL+SHIFT+B
- Delete an e mail message – DEL or CTRL+D
- Reply to message author – CTRL+R

- Reply to all (newsgroups only)– **CTRL+SHIFT+R** or **CTRL+G**
- Forward a message – **CTRL+F**
- Find a message – **CTRL+SHIFT+F**
- Print selected message – **CTRL+P**
- Go to next unread e mail message – **CTRL+U**
- Open selected message – **CTRL+O** or **ENTER**
- Mark a message as read – **CTRL+ENTER** or **CTRL+Q**
- Move between message list, Folders list (if on), and Preview pane – **TAB**
- Go to your Inbox – **CTRL+I**
- Go to a folder – **CTRL+Y**

Shortcuts that can be used in the message window (when viewing or sending):
- Close a message – **ESC**
- Find text – **F3** or **CTRL+SHIFT+F**

Shortcuts that can be used in the message window (when sending messages):
- Check spelling – **F7**
- Insert signature – **CTRL+SHIFT+S**

Finally, here are some **useful CD/DVD shortcuts:**
- Show video in full screen – **ALT+ENTER**
- Switch to full mode – **CTRL+1**
- Switch to skin mode – **CTRL+2**
- Play previous item – **CTRL+B**
- Play next item – **CTRL+F**
- Move focus to search box in library – **CTRL+E**

- Turn shuffle on or off – **CTRL+H**
- Show or hide Classic Menus (menu bar) in full mode – **CTRL+M**
- Create playlist – **CTRL+N**
- Open file – **CTRL+O**
- Play or pause file – **CTRL+P**
- Stop playback – **CTRL+S**
- Rewind video – **CTRL+SHIFT+B**
- Turn captions and subtitles on or off – **CTRL+SHIFT+C**
- Fast-forward through video or music – **CTRL+SHIFT+F**
- Play faster than normal speed (time compression) – **CTRL+SHIFT+G**
- Play at normal speed – **CTRL+SHIFT+N**
- Play slower than normal speed (time expansion) – **CTRL+SHIFT+S**
- Repeat playlist – **CTRL+T**
- Close or stop playing file – **CTRL+W**
- Open Help – **F1**
- Show Classic Menus (menu bar) – **F10**
- Switch to full-screen – **F11**
- Edit media information on selected item in library – **F2**
- Add media files to library – **F3**
- Refresh information in panes – **F5**
- Increase size of album art – **F6**
- Decrease size of album art – **SHIFT+F6**
- Mute volume – **F7**
- Decrease volume – **F8**
- Increase volume – **F9**

EXERCISE 29

WINDOWS EXPLORER

As I've already mentioned, Vista introduced a big number of changes to many applications, including Windows Explorer. In this exercise I will show you a few tips & tricks that can help you when you're working with a large number of files.

When browsing through your files, Windows Explorer shows different columns with details depending on the content of each folder. There are naturally cases when the details shown in each of the columns are not particularly relevant to you at the moment. In such instances you can easily customize the information shown.

To do this, right-click anywhere on the bar that contains the columns with details. You will see a menu with a predefined set of fields – in this case, they refer to music files. Check the details that interest you by clicking on them. If you want to see any other details not included in this list, click on **More**.

Confirm the details that interest you and then click on *OK*. At this point you can also change the order in which they are shown. Select an item from the details list and then click on **Move Up** or **Move Down** until it reaches the desired position.

Choose Details

Select the details you want to display for the items in this folder.

Details:

- ☑ Name
- ☑ Type
- ☑ Rating
- ☑ Year
- ☐ #
- ☐ 35mm focal length
- ☐ Account name
- ☐ Album
- ☐ Album artist
- ☐ Anniversary
- ☐ Artists
- ☐ Assistant's name
- ☐ Assistant's phone
- ☐ Attachments
- ☐ Attributes

Move Up
Move Down
Show
Hide

Width of selected column (in pixels): 80

OK   Cancel

Now, Windows Explorer will show you the information in columns containing only the details which you have selected.

One of the other new actions that you can perform in Windows Explorer is to stack files according to different criteria. For example, I find it helpful to stack files by type. To do this, click on the small arrow from the right of the **Type** column and then click on **Stack by Type**.

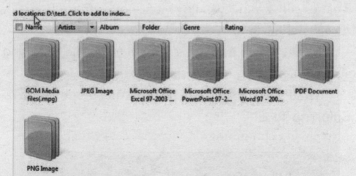

Type ▼	Rating	Year

△ Sort ▦ Group

- ☐ 🗇 GOM Media files(.mpg)
- ☐ 🗇 JPEG Image
- ☐ 🗇 Microsoft Office Excel 97-2003 W...
- ☐ 🗇 Microsoft Office PowerPoint 97-2...
- ☐ 🗇 Microsoft Office Word 97 - 2003 ...
- ☐ 🗇 PDF Document
- ☐ 🗇 PNG Image

☐ Stack by Type

PNG Image
PDF Document
PDF Document
PDF Document
Microsoft Office ...
Microsoft Office P
Microsoft Office E.
Microsoft Office E.
JPEG Image
JPEG Image
JPEG Image
JPEG Image   ☆☆☆☆☆
JPEG Image   ☆☆☆☆☆
GOM Media files(....   ☆☆☆☆☆

Now you will see all the files in stacks ordered by type. The ordering is quite logical: the bigger the stack, the bigger the number of files of that type. When you open a stack, Windows Explorer will show only the files of that type.

As I said before, you can stack files by any criteria: name, file size, rating, or whatever you want. For further exercises relating to Windows Explorer, please look back to the ones beginning on page 85.

EXERCISE 30

SNIPPING TOOL

In Windows XP, the easiest way to take a screenshot was to press the **Print-Screen** key and then **Paste** it in **Paint**. If you wanted to edit the picture and save only a part of the screen you had to lose more time. Paint is OK for basic tasks but, if you want to do more, you really need a better tool. That usually means spending money on better software or time searching for a free or open-source tool.

However Vista includes a gadget called the **Snipping Tool**, designed only for this task.

To find it, go to 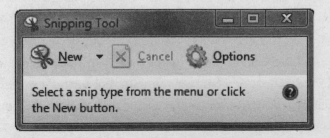 – All Programs – Accessories – Snipping Tool.

When you start it, you will see this Snipping Tool in the middle of your screen while the rest of your desktop will be covered by a transparent white cover and will seem "disabled". That means the tool is in **screenshot mode**. Press the **Cancel** button and everything will get back to "normal".

The Snipping Tool has four capture modes: **Free-form Snip, Rectangular Snip, Window Snip** and **Full-Screen Snip**.

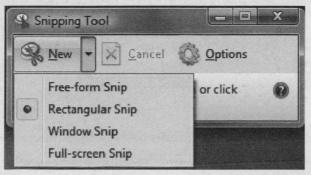

When you select **Free-form Snip**, a small pair of scissors will appear on the screen – you can then select any parts of the screen.

The **Rectangular Snip** mode allows you to draw a rectangle on the screen and capture everything inside it.

In the **Window Snip** mode you just have to select a window with the mouse and the Snipping Tool will take a screenshot of it. The **Full-Screen** mode is even simpler. You just select this mode and the Snipping Tool will capture your desktop, automatically excluding itself from the screenshot.

After selecting the capture mode that you prefer, click on **New**. Once you've taken the screenshot, the result will appear in a new window of the Snipping Tool.

You now have a few options at your disposal. You can Save, Copy, E-mail or Edit your screenshot. You can use the pen, choose its colour and draw something or you can use the highlighter. If you select the eraser you can use it just like an Undo option and remove what you have drawn or highlighted.

After you've edited your screenshot, all you have left to do is to press the Save button in the New menu, type the name of the file, select its location and the format.

For basic Paint tasks you can go back to the exercises commencing on page 94.

EXERCISE 31

PRINTING

In this exercise I will show you how to make your printer work with Vista. It doesn't matter if it's a brand new printer or an old one – by the end of this you will have a working local printer. Local printers are those which you have at home/office, connected directly to the PC on which you are working. After installing the local printer, you can share it with other people that are in your network. They will be able to print but will have to come to your printer to get the pages they printed.

First, start up your PC and plug in the cables that came with your printer. You must have at least one cable which connects the printer to your power outlet and one which connects the printer to your PC. After plugging in all the cables, start the printer. To start the printer, you must locate the right button and press it or you might find it starts automatically. When it does start, it might emit a "warming-up" sound or a small beacon might light up (usually green) on the printer so that you will know that it is working.

Now you have to install the appropriate drivers for your printer, which are programs that drive the communication process between applications and devices – such as your scanner or printer. If your printer is not detected and installed automatically by Vista (which should happen), then you will need to install the drivers yourself. Don't be put off. They can be found on the site of your printer's manufacturer or on the CD that comes with the printer. If you do not have or cannot install the drivers, then follow this procedure:

First, click on the **Start** button and go to **Control Panel**. Next, look in the **Control Panel** window, under **Hardware and Sound,** and click on **Printer**. (If you're back in **Classic View**, check **Printers** or **Printers And Faxes**.)

In the **Printers** window that appears, click on **Add a printer.**

You're not finished yet. In the new window, select *Add a local printer.*

Now choose the type of connection between your printer and your PC from the scroll down list and click on **Next**. If you are not sure what type to choose, read the printer's manual. Most modern printers use **USB cables** to connect to your PC. Older models may use **LPT**. Now you must go to your printer and check the name of the company that made it and the model name & number. In the next window you will see two columns. Go to the **Manufacturer's** column and select the name of the company that produced your printer and in the **Printers** column, select the model. Once you've found it, select it and click on the *Next* button.

Install the printer driver

Select the manufacturer and model of your printer. If your printer came with an installation disk, click Have Disk. If your printer is not listed, consult your printer documentation for compatible printer software.

Manufacturer	Printers
Here you will see the name of the company that made the printer (ex: Lexmark, Hp, etc)	Here you will find the printer's name. (ex: If your printer's name is Lexmark AAA, Hp AAA or "?" AAA you will see just the AAA in this box.)

This driver is digitally signed.
Tell me why driver signing is important

[Windows Update]   [Have Disk...]

[Next]   [Cancel]

If you cannot find your printer, insert the CD that came along with it, click on **Have Disk** and **Browse** to your CD and then click on **OK**. Vista will search for drivers and try to install them. Another option is to click on **Windows Update** and search for drivers on the internet.

Now you can change the printer's name and assign it as a default printer by checking the appropriate option. When done, click on **Next**.

Your printer is now installed and you will duly receive a notification. Click on **Finish** and you are done.

If it hasn't said **You've successfully added...** then click on **Finish**. If Vista warns you that the driver you are planning to install can't be verified, click on **Install this driver software anyway**. However, select this only if the driver you have downloaded is created by the manufacturer of your printer specifically for your model.

If Vista doesn't automatically recognize your printer even after you have installed the driver, the problem might be with the connection cable. Try to plug the printer into another PC (call a friend if you have to) and test it there, to be sure that the connection cable is not damaged.

Alternatively, if you find this all rather daunting, ask whoever installs your PC to install a printer at the same time. For other helpful tips, refer to the exercises beginning on page 97.

EXERCISE 32

CDS, CD-ROMS AND DVDS

Probably one of the first things you'll want to do if you're like me is to play a music CD. You'll find **Windows Media Player 11** is included by default in your installation of Vista and even though it doesn't give you the performance or features offered by more specialized third party solutions, it's all right. So, if you do not want to invest more money on software, here's how to make it work.

Enter your audio CD in your CD/DVD-ROM unit and wait a few seconds. By default, the **AutoPlay** window will pop-up, asking what you want to do:

Now you have two options: you can play all the music found on the audio CD or you can open it and view the files.

To play all the tracks from the CD, choose **Play using Windows Media Player** from the **AutoPlay** menu. If you wish, tick the option **Always do this for audio files** and the next time you insert an audio CD, Windows will automatically open Media Player and play the music found on the CD.

If you want to view the files and only select a few tracks to play, click on **Open folder to view files**. To select files that are not in consecutive order hold down the **Ctrl** key while selecting the tracks with the mouse. To listen to these tracks, click on the blue **Play** button from the right panel or click the right button of your mouse and select **Play**.

Now you know how to play audio CDs with Windows Media Player. There are of course other methods of playing CDs, CD-ROMs and DVDs on your PC, not to mention copying, which you will find explained in exercises starting on page 99.

EXERCISE 33

WINDOWS LIVE MAIL

The other crucial PC boon is to be able to send and receive electronic mail (e-mail). However, Vista can give you some problems. If you try to configure **Windows Mail** to retrieve your e-mail messages from services such as Windows Live Hotmail or MSN Mail, you will always receive the following error message: **Windows Mail no longer supports the HTTP servers used by Hotmail and other web-based e-mail providers.**

That's because, for reasons known only to Microsoft, HTTP forwarding is no longer supported in Windows Mail. You can retrieve your e-mail messages only if you use their newest e-mail client.

This is **Windows Live Mail** and I will show you how to configure it to connect to Windows Live Hotmail and MSN Mail, and access e-mails from your PC.

First, you have to download and install **Windows Live Mail**. Then launch it and look for the **Add an e-mail account** button.

Complete the following fields with your personal information as shown.

When you have entered all information requested, click on **Next**. In the next window check the box that says **Set this account as the default mail account**.

That's all there is to it. Now Windows Live Mail will automatically download all your e-mail messages.

For useful exercises on the workings of e-mail, please see page 113 onwards.

GOODBYE

Once Geraldine had stopped panicking, as she was instructed on the screen saver described on page 31, and had gone through the 33 exercises in this book, she was computer literate. She too can now word-process, manage documents, draw pictures, e-mail and surf the web with ease. She will find that whatever equipment she buys is out-dated by the time her cheque is cashed or her credit card debited, but she can console herself with the thought that any new equipment which saves her a micro-second may take her macro-hours to master.

I wish you the very best of luck.

INDEX

This replaces a Glossary. To find the meaning of a word, look it up here. There's more explanation in the page referred to. On that page, the item referred to here is printed in **bold**, or is a sub-heading.

Arrow, double-headed ↕ or ↔ for dragging a shrunken
 window, 27; for thickening the Taskbar so as to make it
 hold more information, 29; for adjusting the two panes
 of the Explorer window, 86
Arrows on the keyboard, ←↓↑→ , useful for small
 movements of the mouse pointer, 43
Attachment of a File to an e-mail, 115
Auto Arrange icons on Desktop, 84

B
Backspace key ← deletes an automatically printed
 date, 40; deletes text, 44; for going back from Folder to
 parent Folder, 85; to reverse an Enter, 44
Blink, a necessary invitation to type, 13
Blobs on Ruler, adjust margins and indentation, 56
.bmp, see under *extension*
Bold type, on or off, when the **B** button is pressed in or
 toggled out, 41
Boot, a word meaning switch on and wait for the machine
 to warm up or a Program to appear
Box, a rectangle already containing information or empty
 and waiting to have type put in
Broadband, a fast service for connecting to the Internet
Browse, on the **Search Results** window, when looking
 for Files 76
Browse the www = navigate, surf or explore the www
Browser, a dashboard of controls for managing the
 Internet, 108
Bullet, •, 57
Button on the Taskbar, 25; on the Toolbar, 40

play a music CD by putting it into the Drive [D] slot, (see Exercise 18, page 99). CD-ROMs are used to feed software into your machine

Control + Alt + Delete keys, pressed together. A desperate remedy when stuck. See *Stuck* in Index, item F

Control Panel window, for controlling the mouse, 20. Also used for controlling, among other things, the appearance of your Desktop, styles of type and the sounds your PC makes

Copy Here, a choice when dragging with the right-clicker, 73

Copying an e-mail to another e-mail address, 114; automatic copying when moving a File or Folder from C to A, 73

Create shortcuts here, 82

Ctrl + Alt+ Delete, See **Control + Alt + Delete**

Ctrl + Z, same as Undo, 96; useful in Paint, when Undo Button is obscured, 96

Cursor, the blinking mark, 13 and 42; putting it where you want it to be, 43

Cut, Copy and Paste, for moving bits and pieces, 48

Cut, Copy and Paste, for moving whole Files and Folders, 71

D

[D:] Drive, the slot for playing CDs and CD-ROMs, 99

Data, the contents of a File, whether words, pictures or sounds, 62

Date, today's, typed automatically, 59. To see today's date,

G

Games, e.g. Solitaire, 34. Many games are sold as CD-
   ROMs to be added as *Software*

Geraldine, 31

Get the Cursor where you want it to be, 43

Going on-line, 109

Gremlin, a mischievous sprite, 23

Groups, Chatrooms and Blogs, 112

Groups of Files handled as one, 80

H

Hard disk drive C, 68

Hard drive, installing Software onto, 101

Highlighted = changing colour from dull to bright. It
   means you've selected something; Highlighting a
   chunk of text, 46; a single letter, 47; a single word, 46;
   a whole document, 47; for colour printing, 58;
   removing, 47; unwanted when clicking at the left end
   of a line, 50

Home key, 43

http://www, 110

I

Icons apparently misbehaving on the Desktop, 84; useful
   for labelling Buttons, 24

Illegal operation, 60. See *Stuck* below if stuck

Insert key, may go on spontaneously, 44. See *Stuck*, B
   below

Insertion point, chosen by placing the cursor where you
   want to insert something, 48

of the Taskbar, via **start** – **Control Panel** or the button on your keyboard if it has one, 100

Plus sign on Windows Explorer, ⊞ 86

Point, size of print, 52

Portable Storage Device, 122

Print Preview, 97

Print Screen (or **Prt Scn**) key, copies what shows on
     screen, ready for pasting later onto a File

Printing in colour, 58; to start printing, 98; install printer, 166

Program: A set of instructions which tells your computer
     what to do

Q

Question mark, can be moved to a part of a window to
     explain it; on the Mouse Properties window, 21;
     explaining **Match case** in the **Find** window, 56

R

RAM = Random Access Memory, 121

Read only, a state of a File or disk when it can't be
     modified or written over. Floppies can be made *read
     only* by pushing up the little tab at their top corner to
     open the hold. (Push down to close the hole and
     reverse this feature.) If you open a File and its title
     declares, for no apparent reason, that it is *read only*, it
     may simply be that you have already opened it and it's
     quietly lurking on your Taskbar

Receiving e-mail, 115

Recycle Bin, 78; emptying, 79

Register: when installing something, you're often asked to
     register. You don't have to. You don't have to give a
     salesperson your address

and drag it onto Desktop. It appears there as an icon
called *Scrap*. Several *Scraps* dragged into a Folder can
act as a clipboard with a memory of more than one
item

Screen resolution, 103

Screen Saver, **Just don't PANIC, Geraldine**, 31

Scroll bar, 35

Search engines, 111

Search icon on browser, 110

Search results window, 75

Select All, to highlight a whole File, 47; to select all the
files in a Folder, 80

Selecting text = highlighting it

Send to 3½ Floppy [A:], a command on the File menu of
a window listing Files and Folders, 73

Shift key ⇧, for capital letters, 43;

Shortcuts, 150; **Create here**, 82; from Desktop to a File or
Folder, 82; from Desktop to your 3½ Floppy [A:], 83;
from one Folder to another Folder or File, 83; from the
Start menu to a program, 83

Show the Desktop, 29

Single-spacing, 38

Slider, something you can 'drag' sideways or up and
down, 36

Software: information or instructions you feed into
your machine, usually provided as CD-ROMs or
floppy disks. It is of many kinds, such as games, ISPs,
word-processors or encyclopaedias. You can have
such software temporarily available on your screen
just so long as the disk is operating in its slot, or

you can have it installed. If so, you can still use it
after the disk has been removed. Installing
software, 101; word-processing software, 37; uninstall
(Vista) 127

Solitaire, 34

Sounds. Go **start** – **Control Panel – Sounds and
Audio Devices**. To silence sounds, tick **Mute**

Space available on disk, 74

Start Menu is a list of shortcuts to Programs, 83, 132

Start printing, 98

Storing a File = **Save As**, 61

Storing what you've downloaded, 112

Stuck, First aid, 55. Is there something on your screen
asking you to do something, such as clicking **Next** or
Yes? Have you ticked **Mute,** or a Format bar item such
as **right align**? Are there *tabs* on your *ruler?* Are you
Wrapping to **Ruler** or to **Window**?

A. Clear your Taskbar by right-clicking every button
there and clicking **Close** each time

B. If, as you type a character, the one on its right
disappears, you, or a gremlin, may have
unknowingly pressed the **Insert** key. When this
happens, you'll see that pressing the space bar will
delete the character on the right in the same way as
pressing the **Delete** key does. Pressing the **Insert**
key to toggle it off is the cure

C. If your mouse disappears, try pressing **Alt** and the
underlined letter of a menu's name (such as the **F** of
File) and then the underlined letter of an item on
the menu (such as the **P** of **Print**)

of other windows, until a tick remains in the square.
Click the little square opposite **Auto hide** the taskbar
until there is no tick in it. Then click **OK**

Tick ✓ (or check mark in American), 40

Title-bar, at the top of every window, 39

Today's date, typed automatically in WordPad, 59

Toggling off and on, 41

Tool Box, available in the **View** menu of the Paint
Program, 94

Toolbar, available in the **View** menu of WordPad, 40

U

Underline text, 47

Undo last command, a Button on the Tool bar, same as
Ctrl + Z, 48. (This works for three previous commands
in the Paint Program.)

Uninstall. When in trouble with installed software, it
sometimes pays to uninstall and then reinstall. To do
this, go **start** – **Control Panel** – **Add or Remove**
Programs. Scroll the box to find the name of the
program and click it. Then click **Change/Remove**. To
reinstall close all windows, reinsert the disc and start
again

Upper case letter = capital letter, 44

V

View an attachment to an e-mail, 115

View options in Windows Explorer, 86